BRITAIN'S BEST POLITICAL CARTOONS

Dr Tim Benson is Britain's leading authority on political cartoons. He runs the Political Cartoon Gallery and Café which is located near the River Thames in Putney. He has produced numerous books on the history of cartoons, including *Giles's War*, *Churchill in Caricature*, *Low and the Dictators*, *The Cartoon Century: Modern Britain through the Eyes of Its Cartoonists*, *Drawing the Curtain: The Cold War in Cartoons* and *Over the Top: A Cartoon History of Australia at War*.

BRITAIN'S BEST POLITICAL CARTOONS 2018

Edited by Tim Benson

rh
BOOKS

3 5 7 9 10 8 6 4 2

Random House Books
20 Vauxhall Bridge Road
London SW1V 2SA

Random House Books is part of the Penguin Random House
group of companies whose addresses can be found
at global.penguinrandomhouse.com.

Penguin
Random House
UK

Photo on p. 148 © Jesco Denzel/Getty Images

First published by Random House Books in 2018

www.penguin.co.uk

A CIP catalogue record for this book is available from the British Library.

ISBN 9781847948342

Typeset in 11/15.5 pt Amasis MT Light by Jouve (UK), Milton Keynes

Printed and bound in Italy by LEGO, S.p.A.

Penguin Random House is committed to a sustainable future
for our business, our readers and our planet. This book is made from
Forest Stewardship Council® certified paper.

MIX
Paper from
responsible sources
FSC
www.fsc.org
FSC® C018179

INTRODUCTION

Britain's political cartoonists are living through a digital revolution. Over the last 15 years, technology has changed everything: social media has erupted, traditional newspapers have collapsed, and new software has even changed how the cartoons themselves are drawn. It's got many cartoonists wondering about the future. Are we witnessing the end of cartooning as we know it?

Just look at what has happened in the US. Back in the 1980s, 300 newspaper cartoonists were gainfully employed. Today barely a handful is left on the pay roll. And the situation in the UK isn't much better. Of course, we still have a vibrant culture of daily political cartooning in the broadsheet press: *Evening Standard* editor George Osborne recently reinvigorated his opinion pages by bringing back the political cartoon after a hiatus of 13 years. But there are signs that the UK's cartoonists aren't entirely safe. The *Daily Express* and the *Daily Mirror* have now dropped their political cartoons altogether. And since the

Independent abandoned its print edition and went online, its editors have frequently forgotten to update the website's cartoon page.

It's easy to see why. The rise of online news has led to plummeting newspaper circulations and advertising revenues. As the *Guardian*'s Steve Bell puts it, 'I'm my newsagent's best customer when it

The *Montreal Gazette*'s Terry Mosher mourns the death of printed newspapers in the age of the smartphone.

comes to buying newspapers, but my four grown-up kids have never purchased a paper in their lives.' In response, editors have had to find ways to cut costs – and cartoonists are an easy target. According to the American cartoonist and columnist Ted Rall, cartoonists are 'the canaries in the coal mine' for a publication: 'You know a newspaper's in trouble when the staff cartoonist gets the axe.'

Even cartoonists who have held onto their jobs are feeling the squeeze. Where cartoonists would once have been summoned to illustrate major political events such as budgets or general elections, many newspapers now opt for photomontages, which are cheaper and quicker. And the daily political cartoons are being given

Simon Besley suggests that cartoonists might soon go the way of the dodo.

much less space than even a decade ago: broadsheets including the *Guardian* and *The Times* have downsized to a low-cost tabloid format, which inevitably means less room for drawings. According to Steve Bell, even magazines like *Private Eye* and the *Oldie* have started cramping their cartoons: 'They publish the cartoons way too small, giving them no fucking space to breathe!'

As print news has declined, online news has flourished. Almost all newspapers now upload cartoons to their websites. The trouble is, amidst the slew of constantly updated online content, it's easy for a great cartoon to get lost – in fact, at the time of writing, neither *The Times*, *Telegraph* or *Guardian* is featuring a political cartoon anywhere on its online home page. This is a far cry from the golden age of print journalism, as Andy Davey explains: 'You read the whole newspaper and come across, traditionally at least, an image amidst a page of type. Your eyes are drawn to that image because it's strong.' This is simply not the case in the age of online news: 'You have to go and search for a cartoon on a newspaper website, whereas you would be confronted with it in a traditional print newspaper,' he says. Peter Schrank summarises the issue: 'Cartoons do have a problem making their mark and standing out from the relentless flood of images and information.'

The same problem affects cartoonists who take a different path: submitting their work to online-only cartoon blogs, or setting up their own websites. Sadly, most of this work simply gets lost amidst the sheer quantity of satire available online. Type in 'political cartoon' on Google and you get 183 million hits – and the specialist cartoon websites appear several pages into the search. Cartoon blogs simply don't bring in enough revenue to pay their cartoonists, and when they do, it's a pittance. One outcome of this is that many of the new cartoon websites simply aren't up to scratch: thenib.com, a new cartoon-dedicated American blog, is overwhelmed by poor quality cartoons, which made me unsubscribe quickly after signing up. Unable to pay for the crème de la crème of satire, these websites have so far proven to be a cartoon graveyard.

The lack of quality control affects cartoonists on social media, too. There's clearly an appetite on Facebook, Twitter and Instagram for political cartoons; many accounts (mine included) frequently receive hundreds of retweets. But the problem is that most of the satire circulating on social media is of a terrible quality. The cartoons appear to be produced by people with a talent for drawing but without a sense of humour, most of whom obviously have too much time on their hands. As the *Telegraph*'s Bob Moran puts it, 'Today on social media, you find numerous people creating cartoons, gifs, memes, slapping a speech bubble onto a photo of Donald Trump – everyone's a cartoonist!'

This collapse in standards should worry anyone who cares for political cartoons. After all, if our newspapers go the way of the dodo, what will induce top-notch satirists to take up the art form? It's a story all too familiar to anyone acquainted with the history of single-panel 'gag' cartoons. Until the 1980s, gag comics could frequently be found in the likes of *Punch*, *Everybody's*, *Reveille* and *Tit-Bits*; the result was generations of gag artists who were household names, including Pont, Rowland Emett, Fougasse and Michael Ffolkes. Since these magazines went out of print, such artists have largely disappeared. Could something similar happen to political cartoonists?

It's a problem that Britain's finest satirists are all too aware of. Peter Brookes of *The Times* says that declining circulations will likely force newspapers to stop employing top-quality cartoonists. The *Economist*'s Kevin Kallaugher agrees. 'The real threat to the profession during the next decade will be when the present cartooning crew moves on. Few new aspiring cartoonists will likely be inspired to cut their teeth in this niche, challenging and complicated profession,' he says. 'As the seasoned and successful veterans begin to retire, finding experienced replacements will be tricky. This will be a time of danger as future news organisations might be tempted to trim the cartoon position rather than try to fill the large empty shoes with less experienced newbies.'

Nonetheless, most cartoonists believe that their medium will adapt to the online age. According to Steve Bell, 'They are a vital form of communication and as visual satire will always be relevant, they will survive, be it online or in another format.' Indeed, Bob Moran suggests that cartoons are uniquely well suited to the 21st century. 'Good political cartoons are striking images that only require a short span of attention and will be updated by something completely new in less than 24 hours' time,' he says. 'That must stand them in pretty good stead for surviving the digital revolution.'

New technologies haven't just affected the newspapers that publish Britain's cartoons. They have transformed the style of the cartoons themselves. The first rumblings of the coming media revolution were heard in the 1990s, when new printing technology meant that many publications went full colour on every page: suddenly, Britain's cartoonists were expected to work in glorious technicolour.

It was a controversial time. Steve Bell, for example, was disgruntled that he was suddenly expected to work in colour, without being offered a pay rise. Other cartoonists suggested that cartoons had been clearer and funnier before the rise of colour printing: Kevin Kallaugher has continued to work entirely in black and white, even though his publisher, the *Economist*, prints in colour. 'We like the traditional feel that it offers and, in a funny way, the black and white cartoon stands out for its unique look, linking more with the black and white words on the page than the decorative colour that surrounds it,' he says. Stan McMurtry has also remained loyal to the old ways: 'I did say to Paul

As Kathryn Lamb observes, for all the talk of the end of print, our society remains wedded to traditional newspapers – and cartoonists.

The end of greys: until the 1990s cartoons were published in 'half-tone', with cartoonists using a blue pencil or blue wash to indicate the areas to be shaded in.

Dacre, the editor of the *Daily Mail*, that I would be happy to add colour, but he prefers me to continue in black and white. In the last 25 years, I've only ever done one colour cartoon, which appeared in 2014 on the subject of ceramic poppies on Remembrance Day'. Dacre has a point: the great cartoonists of the last century like Vicky and David Low communicated their points masterfully without a drop of colour.

But the controversy over colour cartooning was nothing compared to the current and ongoing debate about digital drawing. These days, cartoonists have the option to create their work on computers and iPads, or tweak it on-screen – something that was unimaginable even 20 years ago. Over in the US, the vast majority of cartoonists have already taken to producing their work digitally. In the UK, the transition to digital technology has been slower: while the *Sun*'s Steve Bright and the *Telegraph*'s Patrick Blower now work digitally, most British cartoonists retain a commitment to pen, ink and paper. That's good news for me. I earn my living from the sale of original cartoons, and so the rise of digital artworks directly threatens my livelihood – there's not much money to be made in selling PDF files.

Why the slow uptake here in Britain? Well, for a number of traditionalists, drawing cartoons on a tablet or computer is nothing short of a betrayal. According to Steve Bright, 'The issue of digital drawing is still quite divisive among many cartoonists, and I know there are some who may never accept that it's not real cartooning unless your hands and desk are covered in ink and paint.' Not surprisingly, those who refuse to adopt new technology tend to be those who started drawing daily cartoons well before the digital age – for them, a cartoon is only authentic if it is completed in 'analogue'. In the words of Peter Brookes, 'For me, drawing on a screen is just not real drawing – it's, in essence, mechanical engineering.' The reason, say these cartoonists, lies in the inimitable aesthetic of ink on paper. In the words of Andy Davey, the artistic process should be 'messy, wet, unpredictable' – characteristics it's impossible to replicate on a screen. *The Times*'s Morten Morland agrees: 'The main reason I like using paper and ink is the line and texture that it produces. I feel it gives much more immediacy and energy to a picture.'

Part of this immediacy comes from the mistakes that arise when you are drawing by hand – after all, you can't just click 'undo' when working in ink. 'Little imperfections betray a process behind it,

which adds to the readers' enjoyment of it,' Morten Morland goes on. The *Independent*'s Dave Brown agrees: 'I like spatter, I like the accidents where the ink splashes, where things are a bit scratchy . . . It doesn't want to look too neat and clean and tidy, because then it loses a bit of edginess.' Indeed, for the veteran cartoonist Ralph Steadman, much of the joy of cartooning comes from making mistakes: 'Of course you'll make a mistake! But there's no such thing as a mistake really. It's just an opportunity to do something else.'

Without mistakes like these, cartoons risk all looking the same – or, in the words of Andy Davey,

The old school versus the new school: the *Daily Mail*'s Stan McMurtry (left) still hand draws his cartoons, whereas the *Sun*'s Steve Bright (right) prefers a tablet.

'flat and soulless'. It's certainly true that digital cartoons have a certain 'look', with consistently thick brushstrokes, flat colours and no rough edges. According to Peter Brookes, 'I know it's a bit of a cliché but a lot of digital work tends to look the same, especially backgrounds . . . Two cartoonists working digitally will produce similar images compared to two cartoonists working in pen, ink and watercolour on paper.' Ralph Steadman agrees: 'The electronic way is a cop out!' Digital cartoons turn artists into 'teeming microbes with no individual characters and unique voices,' he argues.

But above all, the pen-and-ink loyalists say they prefer the pure pleasure of working with traditional materials. Some, like Stan McMurtry, point out the joy of creating a physical archive of 50 years of work. Others speak of their love of using pen and ink: 'There is something about the relationship between the artist and the paper that just isn't there with digital surfaces. It's more real, tangible, dare I say natural,' says Peter Brookes. Kevin Kallaugher says he is a 'mad keen fan of the ancient nib pen' for similar reasons. There is a joy, he says, to the physical sensation of ink against paper: 'There is friction created as the sharp point grabs the surface of the paper creating resistance and depositing the ink with some control. You can feel it working in your fingertips and beyond.' Steve

For cartoonists like Glenn Marshall, who uses watercolours, new technology seems unlikely to rival traditional methods.

Bell makes the case more succinctly: 'I don't want to be hunched over a fucking screen all day. It's just not gratifying.'

Unfortunately for these purists – and for me – ever greater numbers of cartoonists are being won over to the digital side. The *Financial Times*'s Ingram Pinn, who still draws with ink and watercolour, has witnessed the exodus first hand. 'A young art student phoned me saying she was interested in my cartoons and asking if I could tell her how I made them,' he recounts. After explaining his methods, the student still seemed confused: 'She asked how I got the textured effect which I explained was down to the way the watercolour dried on the texture of the Arches paper I use. "No but what program are you using?" she asked, and seemed absolutely astonished when I explained that I didn't draw them on a computer: "Wow, so you actually do them in real life."'

The main reason for the change is convenience. It's much quicker to work on a tablet than on paper. 'Time is probably the most important factor,' says Steve Bright. 'I could still do what I do using traditional tools, but not quickly enough, and with far less versatility and available options that allow

A cartoon by the *Sun*'s Steve Bright demonstrates the distinctive aesthetic of computer-rendered illustrations.

me to resize and reposition the layout of a drawing in seconds.' Nicola Jennings, who colours her images digitally, says that tablets allow her to work more efficiently: 'Since going tabloid the *Guardian* have brought their deadlines forward to 4pm, and 3pm on Sundays, so every minute counts.'

Working digitally also means artists can be more responsive to the needs of their editors. 'I draw for a paper which asserts editorial control over what I do and, inevitably, I am often called to make adjustments to my work,' says the *Telegraph*'s Patrick Blower. 'I concede that something is lost in not having a living, breathing, ink-spattered, tippex-studded, tea-stained piece of artwork but, alas, I've just got too used to the unbeatable advantages of working digitally.' A similar point is made by the *Independent*'s Brian Adcock, who colours his work digitally: 'The experience I now have with digital colouring means I can produce work faster and edit easily if necessary, and if you make as many fuck ups as me that's a useful thing to have.'

Nonetheless, going digital is not always just a pragmatic decision. According to Patrick Blower, in an age of digital media it is 'entirely logical' for cartoons to be produced digitally: 'As more and more readers view my output on backlit digital screens, why not produce the images in the medium in which they're being consumed?' He rails against the 'ancien régime snobbery against digital drawing', saying that there's an inherent value to using computers: 'A digitally made image isn't better or worse, it's just different.' Steve Bright is even more emphatic in his defence of digital cartoons. It's just a matter of keeping up to date, he argues: 'I'm sure if you push my colleagues, they'll tell you nothing beats the sound of a full 100-piece symphony orchestra sitting in their studio while they work – a CD, far less a Bluetooth download, just doesn't cut it . . . How far do you take that argument? Perhaps we should all be drawing cartoons on cave walls using fingers dipped in bull's blood.'

In practice, though, most cartoonists have found a happy compromise between analogue and digital. Amidst the ink-and-paper puritans and the digital evangelists there is a host of cartoonists whose techniques lie somewhere in the middle – utilising digital technology, without going 100 per cent computer-generated. Take the approach of Ben Jennings: 'I still draw all my line work traditionally by hand onto paper. I then scan the drawing into my computer and colour using Photoshop, where I have a variety of brush sets installed along with my own hand-made textures, which I play around with until it looks finished (or until time runs out!).' A similar approach has been adopted by Nicola Jennings, Christian Adams and Brian Adcock, all of whom draw by hand and add texture on-screen. These cartoonists arguably have the best of both worlds.

The evolution of a political cartoon: the *Independent's* Brian Adcock draws on paper and then adds colour using Photoshop.

For truly avant garde cartoonists, it's not enough to produce digital images. They think the 21st century demands fully animated political cartoons, complete with scripts, soundtracks and moving characters. Such animations have already been produced by renowned British cartoonists including Morten Morland, Patrick Blower and Ben Jennings. In America, the genre has been even more successful: in 2010, Mark Fiore won a Pulitzer Prize for his animated editorial cartoons.

Animated satire is hardly a new idea. During the Second World War, Walt Disney produced propaganda cartoons to boost morale on the home front. More recently, TV shows like *2DTV* and *Headcases* have tried to make animated political cartoons accessible to a mass audience – neither, it has to be said, with much success. Perhaps the most bizarre attempt at scripted cartoons came during the 1940s: the BBC asked Britain's most famous political cartoonist, David Low, to make a 'radio cartoon' that would replicate the humour of his drawings. Needless to say, cartoons without images are a bit of a stretch; Low's effort was embarrassingly bad, depending on weak puns and laboured gags. Take the following extract from one 'cartoon' about the Nazi propaganda minister Joseph Goebbels, entitled 'Optimism on the Eastern Front':

ANNOUNCER: *Goebbels deplores pessimism on Eastern Front. Demands that Nazi soldiers look on the bright side. Goebbels to make personal 'cheer up' Tour.*

GOEBBELS [brightly]: Here ve are, back at der front . . .

GERMAN SOLDIER: Ve iss coldt. 2,000 of our comrades were killed yesterday.

GOEBBELS: Grand. More Russian territory occupied.

GERMAN SOLDIER: It's coldt. Und ve were pushed back twenty-five miles yesterday.

GOEBBELS: Splendid! Our victorious troops are returning in triumph.

GERMAN SOLDIER: It's coldt. Und here iss der enemy.

[Rattle of machine guns rapidly rising to crescendo of battle noises. ZIP CRASH BOOM]

GOEBBELS: Wow! Aind't it hot!

Predictably, radio cartoons didn't catch on. But in recent years, mainstream newspapers have dabbled in political animation, usually drawing on the talents of their existing cartoonists. *The Times*'s Morten Morland is one of the best-established satirical animators: he frequently produces animations of about a minute long on topics as varied as UKIP, taxation and Donald Trump. Bob Moran, meanwhile, has produced a touching animation about raising a daughter with cerebral palsy for the *Telegraph*. And the *Guardian* sometimes commissions animated explanations to big political topics.

The logic here is simple: there's simply more money in video content. Publications can charge more to advertise on videos than they ever could on their regular articles, and social media sites like Facebook tend to place videos far above written articles on people's news feeds. So it's not surprising that many publications (and cartoonists) have recently tried to 'pivot to video', producing short films that they hope will get shared on social media.

The drawback is that when political cartoons are animated, they rapidly stop feeling like political cartoons. As the historian Ernst Gombrich says, a static cartoon is a way of condensing 'a complex idea in one striking and memorable image': the cartoonist's point is made almost instantly, and it is this immediacy that gives the image its impact. Animated cartoons are completely different, with the cartoonist's joke gradually evolving over the course of the video.

For this reason most static political cartoonists are sceptical about animations. For them, the joy of cartooning lies in the simplicity of a single drawing. 'It's harder to make it sharp and snappy in

The Times's Morten Morland uses completely different styles in his static cartoons (left) compared with in his animations (right).

animation. I think lengthening the time you look at something actually can reduce the punch,' says Dave Brown: 'with a good political cartoon, you get the gag in seconds.' This simplicity is also hailed by Peter Schrank: 'In the end I think one single strong picture is worth a thousand frames,' he argues. Some cartoonists take a less conciliatory tone – political animations are just 'a blathering fart', says Andy Davey.

In fairness to the animators, very few of them say they are trying to replicate the humour of static cartoons. Static cartoons and animations are simply two different mediums. Just look at the way animations are produced: Morten Morland, who usually works on paper, describes how he has developed a completely distinct method when

WASTE ELIMINATED BY THE CARTOONING MACHINE. PUT IN A NEWS CUTTING AND OUT COMES THE CARTOON — THUS REDUCING COSTS, INCREASING PROFITS AND SAVING A DARNED LOT OF TROUBLE.

Concerns about the death of cartooning are nothing new: here, the early-20th-century master David Low imagines his replacement, the 'cartoon machine'.

creating animations: 'My animated cartoons are done completely digitally . . . Everything needs to be in layers which of course is much easier to do on a computer.' The same is true for the style of the drawings themselves: 'When I first started, about 15 years ago, I tried to make the animated characters look like my painted work, but it just looked like a bad version of it. So instead I developed a completely separate, digital style, which suits the process a lot better.' His comments reveal that, in practice, static cartoons and animations are like chalk and cheese.

In practice, though, the debate between cartoonists and animators is moot: it would be impossible for publications to build animations into their daily news cycles in the way that static cartoons are. For one thing, animations are hugely expensive to produce. And for another, satirical cartoonists simply don't have the time to make them. Sometimes, on a fast-moving news day, a cartoonist may have as little as one and a half hours to complete a cartoon. Animations, on the other hand, usually include 12 drawings per second – meaning that a minute-long animation would require over 700 illustrations. Try producing that in time for a 4pm print deadline.

These days, few political cartoonists think that animation is going to save their art form. This leaves them with no easy answers: torn between collapsing print revenues on one hand and the rise of digital media on the other, the future of cartooning is in doubt. And yet if there's one thing we can count on, it's the ingenuity of the UK's great political cartoonists. After all, the British cartoon tradition stretches from the 19th-century etchings of James Gillray, via wartime masters like David Low, right through to the scathing wit of Steve Bell. It has survived the industrial revolution, print censorship and two world wars. It's a story that encourages many cartoonists to keep the faith: with 200 years of history behind them, political cartoonists might just survive the digital revolution too.

THE CARTOONS

North Korean leader Kim Jong-un tried to demonstrate his country's might through a series of provocative missile tests. In the same week, senior Labour politicians including Jeremy Corbyn, Diane Abbott, John McDonnell and Keir Starmer weighed up whether to back the government's Brexit legislation. According to the cartoonist, 'The world trembled as comedy crazy guy Kim Jong-un fired a rocket over Japan, set off a nuclear test and claimed to have made a launchable H-bomb. Meanwhile, Parliament was due to vote on the EU Withdrawal Bill, which could have been scuppered by Remainer rebel Tory MPs. Here, the Labour politburo educates Kim Jong Corbyn on how the rebellion could, with their help, nuke Theresa May out of Number 10.'

4 September 2017
Andy Davey
Independent

EU officials said they were 'worried' by the UK government's approach to the Irish border after Brexit. All sides were opposed to a 'hard border' with physical checks between Northern Ireland and the Republic of Ireland. But European negotiators said that the solutions proposed by Britain's Brexit team – led by Liam Fox, David Davis, Theresa May and Boris Johnson – 'would not be fair' on the EU.

8 September 2017
Brian Adcock
Independent

10 September 2017
David Simonds
Evening Standard

Jeremy Corbyn compared Theresa May to King Henry VIII, saying she had 'the arrogance of a Tudor monarch'. The prime minister had repeatedly expressed reluctance to give Parliament a vote on the EU Withdrawal Bill. Behind the scenes, the government remained split between Brexiteers like David Davis and Jacob Rees-Mogg and Remainers like Philip Hammond over how best to leave the EU.

WIND OF CHANGE...

Tony Blair called on politicians to oppose Brexit. Speaking on the BBC's *Andrew Marr Show*, the ex-prime minister told MPs to 'find the leadership within yourself to say to people there is a different and better way'. The following day the Met Office issued several extreme weather warnings, predicting winds of up to 70 miles per hour in parts of northern England.

11 September 2017
Morten Morland
The Times

13 September 2017
Steve Bell
Guardian

Theresa May lifted the government's 1 per cent cap on public sector pay, bringing an end to four years of real-terms pay cuts for government employees. A spokesperson for Theresa May said public sector workers 'deserve to have fulfilling jobs that are rewarded', and announced that police and prison officers would receive a 1.7 per cent pay increase the following year. But Labour argued that the decision would make little difference because it only applied to a minority of state employees.

Aung San Suu Kyi, the de facto leader of Myanmar, came under fire for allegedly turning a blind eye to ethnic cleansing in the west of the country. Over the previous month, the Myanmar security forces had forced at least 300,000 Rohingya Muslims to flee their homes. But Aung San Suu Kyi, a Nobel Peace Prize laureate, said it was 'a little unreasonable' to expect her government to have prevented the violence.

16 September 2017
Kevin Kallaugher
Economist

17 September 2017
Morten Morland
Sunday Times

A botched terrorist attack at Parsons Green Underground station, London, injured 30 people. Ahmed Hassan, an 18-year-old Iraqi refugee, had left a bucket containing explosive materials on a rush-hour train on the District line. But the bomb failed to ignite properly and most people on the train escaped unscathed.

Vince Cable, the leader of the Liberal Democrats, said it was 'perfectly plausible' he would be the next prime minister. In a series of interviews during his party conference in Bournemouth, Cable said that his party offered a 'moderate, common-sense alternative' to Labour and the Tories. But many commentators responded that Cable would struggle to halt the decline of the Liberal Democrats, whose vote share had fallen to 7.4 per cent at the 2017 general election.

19 September 2017
Patrick Blower
Daily Telegraph

20 September 2017
Steven Camley
Herald Scotland

Like King Kong before him, Boris Johnson wreaked havoc during a visit to New York – in his case by rebelling against Theresa May's Brexit strategy. According to the cartoonist, 'The prime minister flew to New York in an RAF plane to bring back Boris after he published a three-page personal Brexit manifesto in the *Telegraph*, hinted at resigning and generally undermined her with a 4,000-word article setting out his own post-EU vision.'

Donald Trump said he would use the US's nuclear arsenal to 'totally destroy' North Korea if forced to do so. At a speech to the United Nations, the president labelled Supreme Leader Kim Jong-un a 'rocket man' who was 'on a suicide mission' in his attempts to threaten America. The president later tweeted that while both he and Kim had a 'nuclear button', Trump's was 'a much bigger & more powerful one than his, and my Button works!'

23 September 2017
Gerald Scarfe
Evening Standard

23 September 2017
Bob Moran
Daily Telegraph

Theresa May used a major speech in Florence to outline her vision for the transition period after Brexit. She said there would be a 'status quo' phase after Britain leaves the EU during which the UK would continue to contribute to the European budget. The policy contradicted previous statements made by her colleagues: Boris Johnson, who famously once got trapped on a zip-wire while waving a British flag, had suggested that Britain would be able to immediately stop making payments to the EU.

As the Labour Party conference got underway in Brighton, a report revealed that the majority of delegates attending were supporters of the pro-Corbyn pressure group Momentum. Research by Momentum found that 844 of 1,155 voting delegates supported its proposed reforms to the Labour constitution, designed to make it more likely for future left-wing leaders to be elected. Ben Jennings's cartoon is a pastiche of a raunchy Donald McGill postcard from the 1950s.

25 September 2017
Ben Jennings
Guardian

26 September 2017
Morten Morland
The Times

Shadow Chancellor John McDonnell used his speech at the Labour Party conference to reiterate his commitment to a number of left-wing policies, including scrapping tuition fees and renationalising the water industry. The speech was well received in the conference hall, but was subsequently criticised for including a cornucopia of uncosted policies.

The foreign minister of North Korea, Ri Yong-ho, said that Donald Trump had 'declared war' on his country via Twitter. Ri pointed to a tweet by the US president which warned that Kim Jong-un 'won't be around much longer', saying, 'Given the fact that this came from someone who holds the seat of the US presidency, this is clearly a declaration of war.' The White House dismissed the suggestion, with a spokesperson describing Ri's assertion as 'absurd'.

27 September 2017
Peter Brookes
The Times

'You heard, comrades. I'm ready to be prime minister!'

28 September 2017
Stan McMurtry
Daily Mail

Jeremy Corbyn used his speech at the Labour Party conference to say he was ready to be prime minister. The opposition leader told members, 'We have become a government-in-waiting.' His speech was met with anger by sections of the press: writing in the *Daily Mail*, the historian Dominic Sandbrook said that a Labour administration would 'put our entire national economic future at risk'.

The far-right political party Alternative für Deutschland won seats in the German parliament at a federal election. Their result was widely expected to pull Chancellor Angela Merkel to the right, especially on issues like immigration. 'Of all the politicians currently on the scene I've been drawing Angela Merkel for the longest,' says the cartoonist: 'her posture, those neat trouser suits, the hairstyle. Yes, she has become a bit slicker and there's a harder edge to her face, but essentially she has remained the same. She's very clearly defined. Consequently my drawing of her has become simple and economical. Which is what I'd like to aim for in all caricatures.'

1 October 2017
Peter Schrank
Sunday Business Post

1 October 2017
Chris Riddell
Observer

Leading cabinet members including Liam Fox, David Davis and Boris Johnson arrived in Manchester for the Conservative Party conference. As the event got underway the government was attempting to resolve a dispute involving the aerospace company Boeing, which was putting jobs at risk at an aeroplane factory in Northern Ireland. Government critics said that the dispute revealed the difficulties Britain could have trading after Brexit, arguing it made a mockery of the Brexiteers' much-ridiculed claim that leaving the EU could bring £350 million a week to the British exchequer.

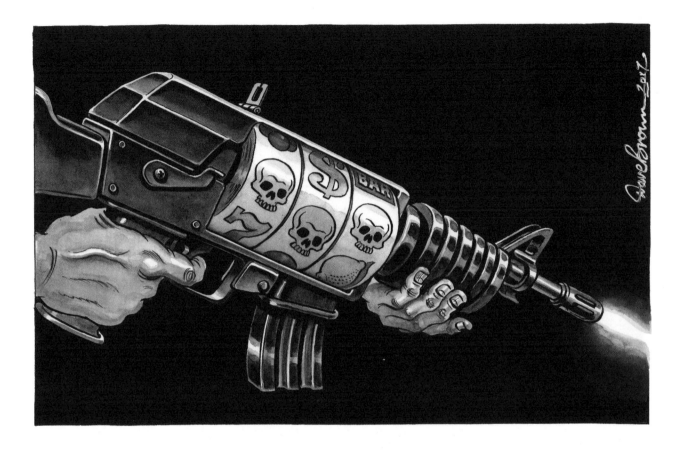

A mass shooting in Las Vegas led to the deaths of 58 people and left 851 injured. Stephen Paddock fired over 1,100 shots from his room in the Mandalay Bay hotel and casino complex, before turning the gun on himself.

3 October 2017
Dave Brown
Independent

OYALTY - THE CONSERVATIVE PARTY'S SECRET WEAPO

RALLY BEHIND THE RIMEMINIST

Belltoons.co.uk

6 October 2017
Steve Bell
Guardian

According to the cartoonist, 'Theresa May, dubbed a "dead woman walking" by George Osborne in the immediate aftermath of the general election, gave a closing speech at the Conservative Party conference in Manchester that achieved new heights of incompetence. A comedian managed to present her with a P45 as she spoke, and as the speech wore on, her voice gave out and was reduced to a croak. Then at the end, as a crowning humiliation, the letters on the slogan on the stage set behind her began to fall off, one by one. Conservative supporters were uncertain whether to rant, rave, laugh or cry.'

Theresa May promised to confront 'uncomfortable truths' exposed by an audit into the way Britain's ethnic minorities are treated. The government report, which investigated the justice system, public services and employers, revealed that white Britons were far more likely to have a job and own a home than those from ethnic minorities. But critics of the government said it needed to look closer to home if it wanted to eradicate racism: Boris Johnson had famously once been forced to apologise for describing Congolese people as 'tribal warriors' with 'watermelon smiles'.

11 October 2017
Dave Brown
Independent

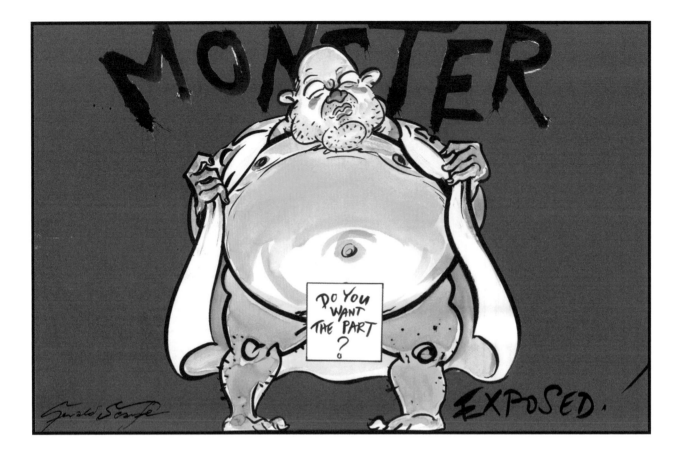

13 October 2017
Gerald Scarfe
Evening Standard

The *New York Times* published accusations of sexual harassment against Hollywood film producer Harvey Weinstein, including allegations that he had promised to help advance women's careers in return for sexual favours.

Jean-Claude Juncker, president of the European Commission, said that Europe was 'grateful' to Britain for its role in Europe's history, including the UK's involvement in ending the Second World War. Sections of the British press said Juncker's comments went against the usual 'don't mention the war' attitude of some European politicians.

14 October 2017
Bob Moran
Daily Telegraph

14 October 2017
Kevin Kallaugher
Economist

Donald Trump threatened to abandon the 2015 treaty between Iran and the world's nuclear powers. The president said he would not continue to certify the deal, in which Tehran agreed to limit its nuclear activities, unless it was altered to toughen the restrictions on Iran. His announcement came just days after he boasted of his high IQ in response to his secretary of state, Rex Tillerson, supposedly calling him a 'moron'.

Pro-Brexit Conservatives called on Theresa May to sack Chancellor Philip Hammond over his approach to leaving the EU. Hammond had caused anger on the Tory right for advocating a 'soft Brexit' whereby Britain would maintain close ties with Europe. In the same week, a heavy storm threatened to bring 70 miles per hour winds to Britain's west coast, reminding Morten Morland of a famous 1987 prediction by the BBC weather presenter Michael Fish: 'Apparently a woman rang the BBC and said she had heard that there was a hurricane on the way . . . Don't worry, there isn't,' Fish famously said on the day before one of the biggest storms in UK history.

16 October 2017
Morten Morland
The Times

22 October 2017
Nicola Jennings
Guardian

Spanish prime minister Mariano Rajoy moved to fire the president of Catalonia, Carles Puigdemont. Puigdemont had held a controversial referendum on Catalan independence on 1 October, which the Spanish government said was unconstitutional. In the words of the cartoonist, 'Carles Puigdemont was subjected to heavy-handed tactics by the Spanish government to suppress Catalonia's vote for independence.'

The World Health Organization revoked the appointment of Robert Mugabe as a 'goodwill ambassador' following an international outcry. Opponents of the appointment had said that the Zimbabwean president was a dictator, and that he had presided over a collapse in the public health of the country – not least as a result of his famously brutal land redistribution programme, which allegedly led to the murder of many farmers.

22 October 2017
Brian Adcock
Independent

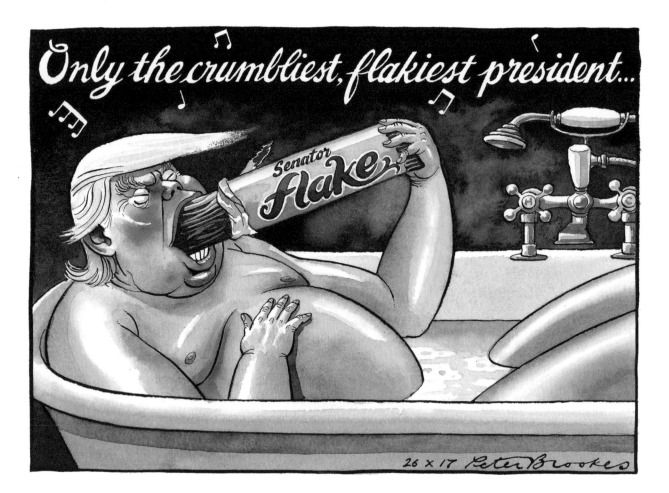

Only the crumbliest, flakiest president...

26 X 17 Peter Brookes

26 October 2017
Peter Brookes
The Times

Jeff Flake, a Republican senator for Arizona, said he would not seek re-election and launched an attack on Donald Trump. He said Trump's behaviour while in office had been 'reckless, outrageous and undignified'. But Trump hit back that Flake was only standing down because he 'had zero chance of being elected' for another term. Over in Britain, the name Flake is perhaps more reminiscent of the Cadbury's chocolate bar – and the iconic ad campaign of a woman eating one in the bath – than of any politician.

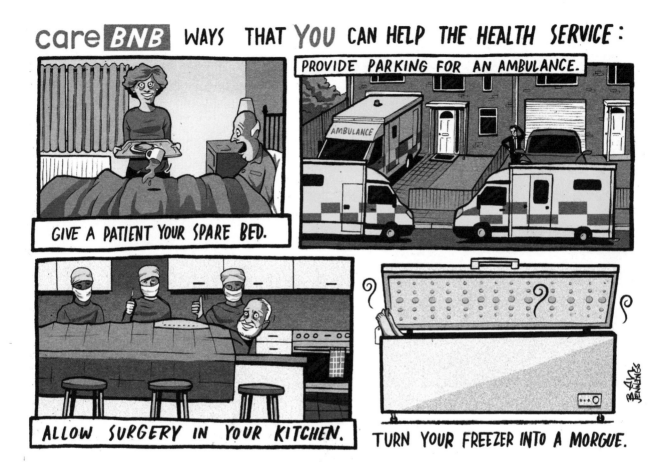

The NHS piloted a new 'Airbnb-style' programme that paid people living near hospitals to 'host' recovering patients. The scheme, designed to free up NHS bed space, was pioneered in Essex by the start-up CareRooms. The company said it would provide a 'safe, comfortable place for people to recuperate', and could pass on up to £1,000 per month to people who rented out a bedroom.

27 October 2017
Ben Jennings
Guardian

The US government released 2,800 previously classified files on the assassination of John F. Kennedy. The president, who is remembered for his line 'Ask not what your country can do for you, ask what you can do for your country', has been the subject of conspiracy theories since being shot by Lee Harvey Oswald in 1963. According to the cartoonist, 'I was looking forward to doing this one, as the contrast between them is so startling. And because I find it irritating that more than 60 percent of Americans still believe that Lee Harvey Oswald didn't act alone. Seems to me there are more important things to worry about. Perhaps this was the moment when the rot set in. In the aftermath of the Kennedy assassination people started distrusting their politicians, their experts, their elites. Not a bad thing in itself, but 55 years later it seems to have landed us in a whole lot of trouble.'

29 October 2017
Peter Schrank
The Times

Theresa May said that allegations of sexual harassment in the Houses of Parliament were 'deeply concerning'. The *Sun* had reported claims that female researchers and aides were using a WhatsApp group to share information about alleged misconduct by MPs and staff. According to the *Sun*, one minister had been branded 'Not safe in taxis' because of his behaviour.

29 October 2017
Ben Jennings
Guardian

FBI officials investigating alleged Russian interference in the 2016 US presidential election announced charges against three of Donald Trump's former campaign officials. Ex-advisers including George Papadopoulos and Paul Manafort were accused of working for a foreign government during the presidential campaign. Trump's critics said the supposed links between his campaign and Vladimir Putin go right to the top of Trump's White House – and that they have the potential to bring down the government.

1 November 2017
Patrick Blower
Daily Telegraph

'I feel a failure as an MP. Fifteen years and I've not had to fend off any inappropriate behaviour.'

Westminster was rocked by more allegations of sexual violence by parliamentarians and their staff. One woman reported that her drink had been spiked with a date rape drug in a bar in the Houses of Parliament, while another said that the Conservative MP she worked for had grabbed her crotch from behind. This cartoon caused a controversy on Twitter, with one user describing its take on sexual harassment as 'horrible, misogynist and not funny at all'.

2 November 2017
Stan McMurtry
Daily Mail

Theresa May attended a dinner with Israeli prime minister Benjamin Netanyahu to celebrate the centenary of the Balfour Declaration, the 1918 statement by the UK government that it would support a 'national home for the Jewish people' in Palestine. According to the cartoonist, 'The Palestinian cartoonist Naj al-Ali was 10 years old in 1948 when he was driven into exile with hundreds of thousands of others by the troops of the newly founded state of Israel. His character Handala, a spiky-haired youth who bears witness to the trials of the Palestinian people and who always appears in back view, is still an iconic figure in the Arab world, despite Ali's murder 30 years ago in London.'

2 November 2017
Steve Bell
Guardian

Leaked documents revealed that about £10 million from the Queen's private estate was invested in offshore tax havens including the Cayman Islands. According to the cartoonist, 'On the rough sketch that I sent to the *Guardian* I had written "by appointment to HM the Queen" underneath the crest on the briefcase. The editor in charge found this "too literal" and asked me to leave it out of the final drawing . . . As this was not a regular gig for me I did as I was told. But it left the cartoon looking a bit vague. A friend thought it was about the UK establishment's complacency in the face of tax avoidance. Which leaves me with this question: should a cartoon make a concise point as well as possible, or is it good enough if it conveys a mood while remaining open to individual interpretations?'

7 November 2017
Peter Schrank
Guardian

"..and then Boris Johnson spoke up on my behalf.."

8 November 2017
Steven Camley
Herald Scotland

According to the cartoonist, 'The foreign secretary endangered the early release of British woman Nazanin Zaghari-Ratcliffe jailed on spying charges while visiting relatives in Iran by remarking that she was just there "teaching journalists".' The UK government's position was actually that Zaghari-Ratcliffe was only visiting Iran on a holiday, and was not teaching journalists. The Iranian regime subsequently quoted Johnson's comments as evidence that Zaghari-Ratcliffe was indeed a spy.

During a state visit to China, Donald Trump lavished praise on Chinese leader Xi Jinping, describing him as 'a very special man'. Having previously attacked the Chinese government, Trump unexpectedly said that he did not begrudge Xi's administration for the Chinese trade surplus: 'After all, who can blame a country for taking advantage of another country for the benefit of its citizens,' he said.

10 November 2017
Peter Brookes
The Times

12 November 2017
Bob Moran
Daily Telegraph

Vladimir Putin and Donald Trump issued a joint statement that reiterated their 'determination to defeat ISIS in Syria'. The two also 'agreed that there is no military solution to the conflict in Syria' and decided to continue to search for a diplomatic resolution, according to the press release. The statement came after the leaders met briefly during the Asia-Pacific Economic Cooperation summit in Vietnam.

Negotiations between Britain and the EU over Brexit fell even further behind schedule, causing European officials to set a two-week deadline to make meaningful progress in the talks. The discussions, led by David Davis with the support of senior politicians including Theresa May, Philip Hammond and Boris Johnson, had stalled for several months over contentious issues including the Irish border.

12 November 2017
David Simonds
Evening Standard

THIS IS NOT A COUP

The Zimbabwean Defence Forces led a coup d'état against the president, Robert Mugabe, but issued a statement saying their moves were 'not a military takeover'. The army sent tanks into central Harare following Mugabe's decision to oust Emmerson Mnangagwa, the second in command within the ruling party ZANU–PF. The coup was widely interpreted as an attempt to prevent the influential first lady, Grace Mugabe, from taking over from her husband as president.

17 November 2017
Ingram Pinn
Financial Times

Theresa May's cabinet agreed to pay the European Union £40 billion as part of the UK's Brexit deal. The decision led to unfavourable comparisons with Margaret Thatcher, who had won a rebate from the European Economic Community in 1984.

19 November 2017
Bob Moran
Daily Telegraph

19 November 2017
Chris Riddell
Observer

Brexit Secretary David Davis reiterated his opposition to paying a 'divorce bill' to Europe. In other news, Chris Riddell accused the retailer John Lewis of copying his 1986 book *Mr Underbed* in its annual Christmas advert, because both feature a child who discovers a cuddly blue monster under his bed. John Lewis responded that most of its advert was 'utterly different'.

Angela Merkel's attempts to build a German cross-party government collapsed, leading to uncertainty about the future of Theresa May's Brexit strategy. According to the cartoonist, 'Although still leader of the largest party in Germany, the chancellor, Angela Merkel, having done worse than expected in the German general election, was unable to form a coalition. Brexit was (and still is) way down her list of priorities as she struggled to stay in power.'

22 November 2017
Steve Bell
Guardian

28 November 2017
Dave Brown
Independent

The Royal Family announced the engagement of Prince Harry to the actress Meghan Markle. Harry, who is sixth in line to the throne, said he was 'thrilled' to be marrying Markle, with whom he had been in a relationship with since mid-2017. Commentators said that the wedding, scheduled for spring 2018, would be a welcome relief from the Brexit chaos engulfing Theresa May's government.

David Davis was accused of misleading Parliament, after he told a select committee that the government had not made impact assessments on the economic consequences of Brexit. In previous select committee hearings Davis had described a number of analyses looking at 'the impact of our exit across the breadth of the UK economy'. Six days after this cartoon was published, Christine Keeler – the woman at the centre of the 1963 'Profumo Affair' that nearly brought down the government, who was famously photographed in the above pose – passed away at the age of 75.

29 November 2017
Dave Brown
Independent

45

THE SPECIAL RELATIONSHIP

1 December 2017
Ingram Pinn
Financial Times

Theresa May criticised Donald Trump for sharing two Islamophobic videos posted by the deputy leader of the far-right group Britain First. The decision to retweet the footage, which purportedly showed Muslims committing crimes in Europe, was described by the prime minister as 'the wrong thing to do'. But Trump hit back via Twitter: 'Don't focus on me, focus on the destructive Radical Islamic Terrorism that is taking place within the United Kingdom,' he said. The row highlighted the difficulty of maintaining the British–American 'special relationship' with such a controversial figure in the White House.

Jeremy Corbyn released a video in which he told the investment bank Morgan Stanley that it was correct to regard him as a 'threat'. The company had warned its clients that a left-wing Labour government would pose a risk to British businesses: Corbyn hit back that he did indeed pose a risk to the banking industry, which consists of 'speculators and gamblers who crashed our economy'. Labour governments have long been described as economically dangerous: in the run up the 1997 general election, Tony Blair's face was famously given satanic eyes in a Conservative election poster entitled 'New Labour, New Danger'.

1 December 2017
Christian Adams
Evening Standard

3 December 2017
Ben Jennings
Guardian

Nigel Farage was accused of hypocrisy for refusing to give up his £73,000-a-year EU pension. The ex-UKIP leader is entitled to the money for his work as a member of the European Parliament. On his LBC show, Farage rejected the accusation: 'I've just voted to get rid of my job . . . I was the turkey that voted for Christmas. How is that hypocrisy? If it was hypocrisy, I'd have said we should stay in the EU.'

Former police officers alleged that 'extreme' pornography had once been found on a computer belonging to the first secretary of state, Damian Green. They said that the material had been discovered in Green's computer in a police raid on Parliament during a 2008 investigation into Home Office leaks. But Green, a close ally of Theresa May, strongly denied the allegation that he had downloaded or watched the material, and Metropolitan Police Commissioner Cressida Dick said that the policemen's allegation was a breach of Green's confidentiality.

4 December 2017
Steve Bright
Sun

ANOTHER FINE MESS...

6 December 2017
Peter Brookes
The Times

The first minister of Northern Ireland, Arlene Foster, scuppered Theresa May's proposals for a new Brexit arrangement at the Irish border. EU leaders had hinted that they had come to an agreement, whereby Northern Ireland would remain part of the European Single Market. But Foster, whose Democratic Unionist Party supports the government in Parliament, rejected the proposals at the last minute. Here, Foster re-enacts a famous scene from the film *Another Fine Mess* – except with Laurel & Hardy's famous bowler hats incorporated into the uniform of Northern Irish Protestant group the Orange Order.

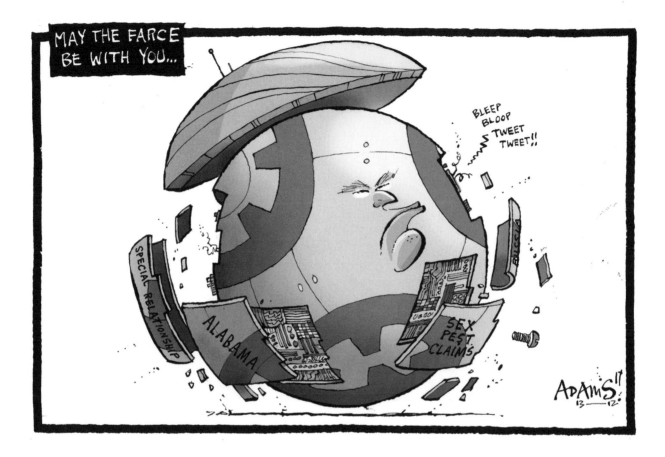

Donald Trump claimed that sexual harassment accusations against him were a conspiracy organised by the Democratic Party. He also came under fire after his preferred candidate for the Alabama Senate election, the former judge Roy Moore, dramatically lost the election. Meanwhile, *Star Wars: Episode VIII – The Last Jedi* opened in British cinemas.

13 December 2017
Christian Adams
Evening Standard

16 December 2017
Ben Jennings

i

Walt Disney bought most of Rupert Murdoch's film business, 21st Century Fox. The purchase included a 39 per cent stake in UK-based broadcaster Sky, as well as Fox's TV and film studios. The move brought iconic Disney creations like Mickey Mouse under the same umbrella as hit TV shows like *The Simpsons*.

The EU announced that Brexit talks could shift from Phase 1 to Phase 2, the period of negotiations that would cover the long-term relationship between the UK and Europe. According to the cartoonist, 'The EU headed into the next phase thinking they were in a very strong position. After her very own "annus horribilis" of a botched election, conference nightmare, cabinet resignations and Commons defeats, May was just hoping to get to Christmas still in post. She also wanted to unite her party after some vicious in-fighting including death threats to Brexit "traitors". Frying pans, fires and Christmas turkeys came to mind.'

16 December 2017
Andy Davey
Independent

20 December 2017
Peter Brookes
The Times

The retailer Toys R Us teetered on the verge of collapse, putting 3,200 UK jobs at risk. The company had struggled to adapt to the rise of new online toy sellers like Amazon. Meanwhile, Tory politicians including Michael Gove, Boris Johnson, Theresa May and David Davis clashed over how best to approach the next phase of Brexit negotiations.

The EU's chief Brexit negotiator, Michel Barnier, struck a blow to Theresa May's hopes of a bespoke deal for Britain's financial services companies. Theresa May had reportedly hoped for a bespoke 'passport' for the City of London that would give it special access to the European Single Market. But Barnier said, 'There is not a single trade agreement that is open to financial services. It does not exist.'

20 December 2017
Brian Adcock
Independent

21 December 2017
Steve Bell
Guardian

Republicans in the US Congress passed the most sweeping tax reforms in decades, slashing taxes for corporations and the wealthy. Donald Trump said that the reforms proved he was 'making America great again'. But senior Democrats strongly criticised the bill, with Senator Elizabeth Warren tweeting, 'Let's call this out for what it is: Government for sale.'

First Secretary of State Damian Green was sacked from the cabinet, after an inquiry found he had made 'inaccurate and misleading' statements about allegations that pornography had been found on his computer. Green had denied downloading or viewing the material, and said the police had 'never suggested' that improper material was found. But after the inquiry, Green acknowledged that he had in fact been informed about the discovery of the material in 2008, and apologised 'that my statements were misleading on this point'.

22 December 2017
Dave Brown
Independent

According to the cartoonist, 'Donald Trump formally announced the United States' recognition of Jerusalem as the capital of Israel, reversing nearly seven decades of American foreign policy, and ordered the planning of the relocation of the US embassy from Tel Aviv to Jerusalem. The United States Capitol dome eclipses the Dome of the Rock, thereby eclipsing Arab sensibility.'

27 December 2017
Nicola Jennings
Guardian

Barack Obama took a swipe at Donald Trump in his first interview since leaving the White House. Obama said that social media was stopping normal conversations and he encouraged people to meet offline – widely interpreted as a dig at his Twitter-obsessed successor as president. According to the cartoonist, 'Taking on this kind of idea always presents a risk. The danger was that either it wouldn't look like a wave, or it wouldn't look like Trump. I hope I just about got away with it.'

28 December 2017
Peter Schrank
Guardian

NEW YEAR'S RESOLUTIONS

Seamus Jennings 31.12.17

31 December 2017
Seamus Jennings
Daily Telegraph

Theresa May ended the year in a precarious position, with challenges to her leadership coming both from Jeremy Corbyn's Labour Party and from dissenting members of her own cabinet like Boris Johnson. She insisted in an interview that she would spend 2018 'getting on with the job'.

UNRAVELLING ..?

Violent protests against the government in Iran left 21 people dead. The demonstrations, which had been sparked by price rises and allegations of corruption, were the largest to hit the nation since 2009. But Supreme Leader Ayatollah Ali Khamenei said that the protests had been stirred up by the enemies of Iran.

3 January 2018
Dave Brown
Independent

Tony Blair launched an attack on Jeremy Corbyn's approach to leaving the EU, arguing it was 'confusing' and 'mistaken'. An outspoken opponent of Brexit, the former prime minister published an article on his website saying, 'Because the Labour Party is saying that we too would do Brexit, we cannot attack its vast distractive impact.' But Corbyn's allies said that Blair's intervention was unhelpful, especially considering his unpopularity with the British public: in one 2017 poll, the former Labour leader had an approval rating of only 21 per cent.

5 January 2018
Bob Moran
Daily Telegraph

Donald Trump attempted to prevent the publication of a new book about life inside his administration. Embarrassing allegations made in Michael Wolff's *Fire and Fury* – including that the president's love of McDonald's burgers resulted from his fear of being poisoned – had appeared in the press. In response, White House lawyers sent a letter to Wolff's American publisher demanding that the book was cancelled. Trump said that the book was 'phony' and that it was 'full of lies, misrepresentations and sources that don't exist'.

5 January 2018
Christian Adams
Evening Standard

8 January 2018
Morten Morland
The Times

Every NHS hospital in Britain was ordered to postpone all non-urgent surgery scheduled for January. The announcement was a response to the worst winter health crisis in decades, in which doctors struggled to find enough beds for patients. It came during a bad week for the government: Theresa May was also forced to abandon an unpopular pledge to let Parliament vote on legalising fox hunting.

Theresa May reshuffled her cabinet. She was accused of weak leadership following reports that the health secretary, Jeremy Hunt, convinced her in the course of their meeting not to demote him. Meanwhile, the Winston Churchill biopic *Darkest Hour* was released in the UK. Film critics lavished praise on its star, Gary Oldman, especially for his re-creation of Churchill's 'We shall never surrender' speech.

10 January 2018
Peter Brookes
The Times

14 January 2018
Chris Riddell
Observer

Nigel Farage said he was considering advocating a second referendum on the EU. The former UKIP leader said it was the only way to stop the 'whinging and whining' of Remain campaigners, even though it was the 'last thing' he wanted. Meanwhile, Theresa May said her government planned to eradicate all avoidable plastic waste within 25 years. 'I think people will be shocked at how today we allow so much plastic to be produced needlessly,' she said.

UKIP suspended Jo Marney, the partner of party leader Henry Bolton, after she made racist remarks about Prince Harry's fiancée. The *Mail on Sunday* had uncovered text messages sent by Marney in which she said that Meghan Markle, who is mixed race, would 'taint' the Royal Family. Marney apologised but said that her messages had been taken out of context. In America, meanwhile, Donald Trump was forced to deny being racist after he reportedly called African nations 'shithole countries'.

15 January 2018
Christian Adams
Evening Standard

17 January 2018
Steve Bell
Guardian

Theresa May's government announced an investigation into the conduct of directors at the construction company Carillion, which went into liquidation on 15 January. Commentators had suggested that the collapse of the company was in part down to 'fat cat' executives who had mismanaged it while taking home huge pay cheques – according to Steve Bell, a situation comparable to the classic farce *Carry On Up the Khyber*.

French premier Emmanuel Macron agreed to loan the Bayeux Tapestry to the British Museum. Macron, who has faced criticism for his 'egotistical' style of leadership, conceded to the move during a state visit to the UK, in which he also convinced Theresa May to accept a £45 million bill for France's efforts in preventing illegal immigrants entering the UK.

17 January 2018
Christian Adams
Evening Standard

23 January 2018
Morten Morland
The Times

The national executive committee of UKIP passed a vote of no confidence in its leader, Henry Bolton, after a series of damaging allegations appeared in the press about his partner. Former UKIP leader Nigel Farage said that Bolton had been 'pretty stupid' in his handling of the allegations. The incident was the third leadership crisis for UKIP in quick succession, with two leaders – Diane James and Paul Nuttall – already having resigned over the previous 18 months.

Boris Johnson reportedly called for a cash boost for the NHS during a fraught cabinet meeting. The foreign secretary was widely quoted as being 'very concerned' about healthcare funding following a visit to his constituency hospital. But members of the government including Theresa May rebuked Johnson for failing to keep the proceedings of cabinet meetings confidential.

24 January 2018
Dave Brown
Independent

FLASH...

Pay CHARITY

£2,000,000

Signed Presidents Club

Ben Jennings

25 January 2018
Ben Jennings
Guardian

A *Financial Times* investigation revealed widespread sexual harassment at a charity fundraiser in the City of London. The event, organised by the 'Presidents Club', was only open to men and was billed as the 'most un-PC event of the year'; female 'hosts' were groped and propositioned throughout the night.

A cabinet minister called for the 'left, right and centre' of the Conservatives to 'come together in a spirit of mutual respect'. David Lidington, minister for the Cabinet Office, made his comments after a tumultuous week in which the Conservatives appeared openly divided over their policy agenda, with backbencher Jacob Rees-Mogg criticising Chancellor Philip Hammond over his approach to Brexit, and Boris Johnson clashing with Theresa May over NHS spending.

29 January 2018
Brian Adcock
Independent

A leaked government report suggested that leaving the EU will make the UK worse off. The analysis modelled the economic effect of three different kinds of Brexit deal, and concluded that each of them would lead the economy to grow more slowly than if Britain remained in Europe. The news was especially damaging to Theresa May because her ministers had previously maintained that there were no comprehensive impact reports about Brexit.

31 January 2018
Steve Bell
Guardian

'Remind me, Grandad. What was a Nazi?'

A group of left-wing activists stormed a Winston Churchill-themed café in north London. Blighty UK, which is decorated with Spitfire posters and Churchill mugs, was denounced for its 'unashamed colonial and gentrifying presence' by the activists, who cited racist comments made by Churchill in the early 20th century. There was an immediate backlash to the protestors, with Boris Johnson calling the protest a 'disgraceful attack on our finest ever wartime leader'.

31 January 2018
Stan McMurtry
Daily Mail

1 February 2018
Dave Brown
Independent

Theresa May came under fire for 'kowtowing' to the Chinese government during an official visit. Campaigners had hoped that the prime minister would make China's human rights record a central part of her visit, but the *Global Times*, a state-run media outlet, praised her for ignoring their 'noise and nagging' in order to 'sidestep' the issue.

Donald Trump called for America to come together as 'one team, one people and one American family' at his first State of the Union address. The speech offered an 'open hand' to Democrats to work together in making policy, after a year of aggressive bipartisanship in Congress. Trump's critics said that the comments were disingenuous considering his divisive approach to policymaking: a *Washington Post* editorial asked, 'Have a president's words ever rung more hollow?'

2 February 2018
Kevin Kallaugher
Economist

FROSTY WEEK AHEAD...

CUSTOMS UNION

6·2·18 MORLAND

6 February 2018
Morten Morland
The Times

Theresa May chaired a meeting of senior ministers to try to heal the divides in her cabinet over Brexit. Boris Johnson, Philip Hammond, David Davis and other frontbenchers spent over two hours attempting to resolve how closely the UK should be linked to Brussels after leaving the EU. Meanwhile, the Met Office issued warnings about a week-long cold spell that was about to descend on England.

Theresa May gave a speech to mark 100 years of women's suffrage. The prime minister paid testament to early-20th-century suffragettes who, under the slogan 'Deeds Not Words', chained themselves to the railings outside 10 Downing Street and went on hunger strike. The speech came at a difficult time for the prime minister, who had been accused of weakness over her muddled Brexit strategy.

6 February 2018
Christian Adams
Evening Standard

8 February 2018
Peter Brookes
The Times

Donald Trump asked the Pentagon to organise a military parade in Washington D.C., having been impressed by the French Bastille Day celebrations on a state visit the previous July. Trump described the festivities in Paris as 'one of the greatest parades I've ever seen', adding, 'We're going to have to try and top it.' Democrats said that Trump's plans made him sound like a dictator, with Representative Jackie Speier telling CNN, 'We have a Napoleon in the making here.'

The government of Haiti suspended Oxfam's operations in the wake of a number of claims of sexual misconduct by its aid workers. The allegations dated back to the aftermath of the 2010 earthquake, when Oxfam staff were said to have taken advantage of displaced Haitians.

12 February 2018
Brian Adcock
Independent

THE EMPEROR'S OLD CLOTHES...

YOU'VE SOILED IT !!

MANTLE of MANDELA

14 February 2018
Dave Brown
Independent

The ruling party of South Africa, the African National Congress, asked President Jacob Zuma to resign. Zuma had been plagued by accusations of corruption and in 2016 was ruled to have violated the constitution for spending government money on renovating his private home. Zuma, who had frequently compared himself to former president Nelson Mandela, vehemently denied the allegations.

A school shooting in Parkland, Florida, left 17 people dead. The attack at Stoneman Douglas High School, undertaken by a former student of the school with a semi-automatic weapon, was one of the deadliest school shootings in US history.

15 February 2018
Ben Jennings
Guardian

18 February 2018
Nicola Jennings
Guardian

According to the cartoonist, 'At the Munich security conference Theresa May had the nerve to use UK security and intelligence expertise as a bargaining chip in Brexit negotiations.' The prime minister told leaders of the European community including Angela Merkel that they needed British expertise to keep safe.

Several Russian citizens were charged with meddling in the 2016 US presidential election. An FBI investigation alleged that 13 Russians had created fake social media accounts and organised political rallies, with a view to 'supporting the presidential campaign of then-candidate Donald J. Trump' and 'disparaging' his opponent, Hillary Clinton. The indictments were the latest allegations of collusion between Trump supporters and the Kremlin, here represented by the traditional Russian bear.

18 February 2018
Brian Adcock
Independent

Jeremy Corbyn described allegations that he gave information to a Communist spy during the Cold War as 'ridiculous smears'. Both the Labour leader and Czech security officials dismissed claims in the *Sun* that he was a paid informant of foreign intelligence. According to the cartoonist, 'Jeremy Corbyn was dragged into a farcical Communist spy scandal. Just another week in British politics.'

18 February 2018
Scott Clissold
Sunday Express

Survivors of the Florida school shooting met with Donald Trump in the White House to call for tighter gun control. The president suggested the best way to prevent shootings was to allow teachers to carry concealed weapons, a policy that has long been advocated by the controversial pro-gun lobby group the National Rifle Association (NRA).

18 February 2018
Chris Riddell
Observer

19 February 2018
Brian Adcock
Independent

Henry Bolton was ousted as leader of UKIP after a slew of allegations about his private life. His dismissal forced the beleaguered party to find its sixth leader in just 18 months. Many commentators suggested that Bolton's removal demonstrated the continued influence of ex-leader Nigel Farage, who had been a vocal critic of Bolton's leadership.

LABOUR'S U-TURN

A CUSTOM UNION

Jeremy Corbyn clarified the Labour Party's position on Brexit, coming out in favour of a permanent customs union with Europe. The move increased the divide between the government and the opposition on how to leave the EU, and raised the possibility of Theresa May being defeated in an upcoming vote in Parliament. Meanwhile, the February cold spell continued.

26 February 2018
Christian Adams
Evening Standard

28 February 2018
Peter Brookes
The Times

Donald Trump criticised the police who arrived at the scene of the Parkland school shooting for failing to apprehend the culprit more quickly. Speaking to a gathering of 39 state governors at the White House, Trump said, 'I'd run in there even if I didn't have a weapon,' and described the police's inability to stop the shooting as a 'disgrace'.

Russian premier Vladimir Putin requested a 'humanitarian pause' in the Syrian government's bombardment of the rebel-held territory of Eastern Ghouta. Putin, an ally of Syrian president Bashar al-Assad, called for the daily ceasefire after over 560 people were killed in the region in the course of just eight days. Critics of the Russian leader said his 'pause' was insufficient, considering the Kremlin would still support Assad's brutal repression of dissidents.

2 March 2018
Gerald Scarfe
Evening Standard

Politicians from across the political spectrum, including Tory backbencher Jacob Rees-Mogg and former prime ministers John Major and Tony Blair, criticised Theresa May's Brexit strategy. According to the cartoonist, 'It was Oscar week and the deep divisions over Brexit in both the Conservative and Labour parties continued to take centre stage. The one thing all the warring factions seemed to agree on was Theresa May needed to up her performance and change her script.'

4 March 2018
Scott Clissold
Sunday Express

Roger Bannister, the first man to run a mile in under four minutes, died at the age of 88. The news came in the same week that MPs concluded that the cyclist Bradley Wiggins had 'crossed an ethical line', by using performance-enhancing drugs while preparing for the Tour de France in 2012. The two stories led to discussion of how much Britain's sporting culture had changed since Bannister set his record in 1954.

6 March 2018
Ben Jennings
Guardian

North Korean premier Kim Jong-un would meet with US President Donald Trump, it was announced. The news came in the wake of a war of words between the two leaders over North Korea's nuclear weapons programme. In 2017 Donald Trump had described Kim as a 'rocket man', and Kim had retaliated that the US president was 'mentally deranged' and a 'dotard'. Ben Jennings's image recreates an iconic David Low cartoon from 1939, *Rendezvous*, which depicted Adolf Hitler meeting with Joseph Stalin during a similarly uneasy truce.

10 March 2018
Ben Jennings
i

Philip Hammond said there was a 'light at the end of the tunnel' for the UK's public finances, but commentators responded that Brexit was bound to hamper Britain's economic recovery. According to the cartoonist, 'This was one of those jobs we all dread. I had a very difficult time getting approval for my ideas that day. The comment editor had already turned down two rough sketches on two different subjects, and with a 4pm deadline at the *Guardian*, time was getting very tight. At around 12.30pm I finally got this idea approved . . . With hindsight I should have drawn Hammond plastered over the front of the engine, with the caption split between the two frames. But I just didn't have time to reflect.'

13 March 2018
Peter Schrank
Guardian

ROBUST RESPONSE...

13·3·18

A former Russian spy was nearly killed in a nerve agent attack in Salisbury, Wiltshire. The British government said that it was likely that Vladimir Putin's Kremlin was behind the attack, with Foreign Secretary Boris Johnson promising a 'robust' response if Russian involvement was proven. In other news, the comedian Ken Dodd died at the age of 90. One of the best-known entertainers of his generation, Dodd was famed for the iconic feather dusters – or 'tickling sticks' – that he used as props during his performances.

13 March 2018
Morten Morland
The Times

BRIGHTY
(GOD SPEED, PROFESSOR!)

The physicist Stephen Hawking died at the age of 76, following a 50-year battle with motor neurone disease. The British scientist was famed for his research into black holes and relativity, and also for his atheism. 'There is a fundamental difference between religion, which is based on authority, [and] science, which is based on observation and reason,' he once said: 'Science will win because it works.'

14 March 2018
Steve Bright
Sun

17 March 2018
Kevin Kallaugher
Economist

Donald Trump fired his secretary of state, Rex Tillerson. The former ExxonMobil chief had had a series of public clashes with the White House since his appointment in 2017. Trump, who in January had described himself as a 'genius', said that Tillerson's dismissal was down to disagreements on issues like Iran and trade policy: 'We got along actually quite well, but we disagreed on things,' said the president.

ONE MAN, ONE VOTE...

Vladimir Putin won a landslide victory in the Russian presidential election. The incumbent leader won 75 per cent of the vote, securing a fourth term in office. Critics of the regime said that Putin had rigged the election, and that his victory was the only possible outcome.

19 March 2018
Morten Morland
The Times

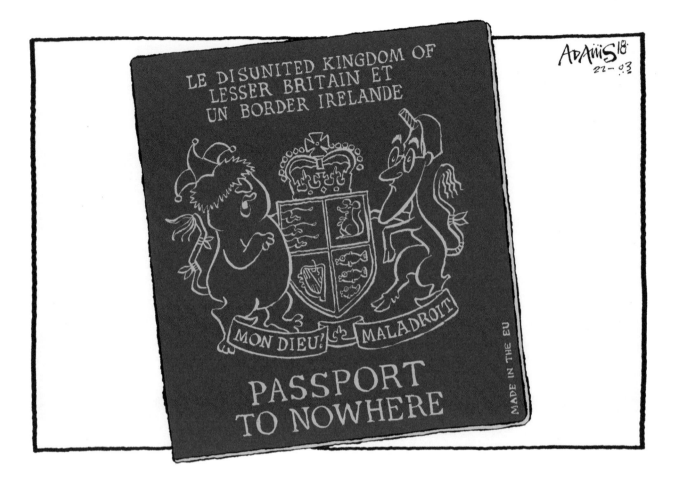

22 March 2018
Christian Adams
Evening Standard

The contract to manufacture British passports was awarded to a Franco-Dutch company. Pro-Brexit MPs including Boris Johnson and Jacob Rees-Mogg had campaigned for the passport to revert to its traditional blue colour from its current burgundy. But many were disgruntled when it was announced that the new version will be manufactured in France by the digital security firm Gemalto.

Facebook founder Mark Zuckerberg came under fire for allowing a controversial political consultancy to access millions of users' data. Cambridge Analytica harvested the data of millions of accounts, then supplied it to supporters of Donald Trump to use in their campaigns. Zuckerberg said that the social network had 'made mistakes', and that he was 'really sorry' for letting 'rogue apps' misuse the site.

25 March 2018
Chris Riddell
Observer

27 March 2018
Patrick Blower
Telegraph

Jeremy Corbyn acknowledged the existence of 'pockets' of antisemitism within the Labour Party, saying he was 'sincerely sorry' to the Jewish community. In a statement, the opposition leader said his party 'will not tolerate any form of antisemitism that exists in and around our movement'. But Corbyn's critics pointed out that many of those accused of antisemitism were vocal supporters of the current party leadership.

The adult film actress Stormy Daniels alleged that she had had an affair with President Donald Trump in 2006. She also said that when she attempted to go public with the story, a stranger approached her and warned her to 'leave Trump alone'. Trump denied the affair, and his lawyers moved to sue Daniels for breaking a non-disclosure deal signed before the 2016 presidential election.

27 March 2018
Dave Brown
Independent

Boris Johnson was reprimanded by the speaker of the House of Commons, John Bercow, for comments he made to the shadow foreign secretary, Emily Thornberry. Johnson had referred to Thornberry as 'Lady Nugee', because she is married to the High Court judge Sir Christopher Nugee. But Bercow rebuked Johnson, saying, 'We do not address people by the titles of their spouses.' Meanwhile, the cricket world was stunned when members of the Australian team were found guilty of 'tampering' with the ball during a match against South Africa. Here, Steve Bell brings the stories together in a re-creation of the 1878 William Frederick Yeames painting *And When Did You Last See Your Father?*.

28 March 2018
Steve Bell
Guardian

Jeremy Corbyn was criticised for defending an antisemitic mural that had been painted in east London in 2012. The original mural, which is parodied in Peter Brookes's cartoon, depicted men with exaggeratedly 'Jewish' features playing a board game on the backs of the world's poor. Corbyn, who had opposed the removal of the painting in 2012, issued a statement saying that he now realised it was 'deeply disturbing'. Senior Labour MPs including Corbyn, John McDonnell and Diane Abbott, as well as high-profile supporters including Len McCluskey, Christine Shawcroft and Ken Livingstone, had previously come under fire for turning a 'blind eye' to racism in the party.

30 March 2018
Peter Brookes
The Times

TO RUSSIA WITH LOVE

31 March 2018
Ingram Pinn
Financial Times

Countries from around the world expelled Russian intelligence officers in response to the Salibsury nerve agent attack allegedly carried out by the Kremlin. The US, Australia, Canada and 23 European countries expelled over 150 Russian operatives. Russian premier Vladimir Putin responded by vowing to expel western diplomats in retaliation.

Jeremy Corbyn faced renewed criticism over his handling of antisemitism allegations within the Labour Party. According to the cartoonist, 'I drew this on Easter Sunday, during a bank holiday weekend of truly awful weather. It seemed to me that the papers were already flooded with cartoons on the subject, and I didn't relish the prospect of adding yet another one. Not least because the issues here are complex. Antisemitism, the fear of it, and a critical stance towards Israel's treatment of the Palestinians get uncomfortably mixed up in the minds of both supporters and critics of Israel's policies. Such is the case here. So I was glad to reduce it to a comment on Jeremy Corbyn's competence.'

2 April 2018
Peter Schrank
The Times

4 April 2018
Nicola Jennings
Guardian

A new law requiring companies to publish information about the pay gap between men and women sparked renewed concern about the 'glass ceiling' facing female employees. The data revealed that in large companies, women are on average paid 9.7 per cent less than men. Meanwhile, Theresa May faced another tough week dealing with the fallout from the nerve agent attack in Salisbury.

LET THE GAMES BEGIN!

Jeremy Corbyn criticised Boris Johnson, the foreign secretary, for 'misleading' the public over the poisoning of a former Russian spy. Johnson had said experts were 'absolutely categorical' that the poison came from Vladimir Putin's Russia – a claim the Labour leader said was 'a bit of an exaggeration'. Meanwhile, the 2018 Commonwealth Games got underway in Australia.

5 April 2018
Christian Adams
Evening Standard

5 April 2018
Seamus Jennings
Daily Telegraph

Donald Trump introduced $100 billion of additional trade tariffs against China. In response, Beijing unveiled their own list of tariffs targeting a wide range of American imports. Meanwhile, a sensational overhead kick by Cristiano Ronaldo led his team, Real Madrid, to a 3–0 victory over Juventus in the Champions League quarter-final.

Leaked Home Office documents suggested that cuts to the police had probably contributed to an increase in violent crime. The government report highlighted a fall in the number of police officers since 2014, noting that 'resources dedicated to serious violence have come under pressure' which could have 'encouraged offenders'. Meanwhile, mayor of London Sadiq Khan backed giving the police 'targeted' stop and search powers against individuals they think are carrying weapons.

8 April 2018
Brian Adcock
Independent on Sunday

THE STATE OF PLAY...

9 April 2018
Morten Morland
The Times

Seventy people were killed in a chemical weapons attack in Douma, Syria. The attack was widely attributed to the Syrian army, and led to international criticism of Syrian president Bashar al-Assad and his Russian ally Vladimir Putin.

A group of Eurosceptic campaigners announced their plans for a 'Museum of Brexit'. The museum would include Brexit memorabilia and documents, in order to 'recall, for future generations, the story of the struggle for the United Kingdom's independence'. Its organisers, who included former executives at UKIP and the pro-Brexit campaign Vote Leave, called for items including placards, badges, posters and campaign rosettes that could serve as exhibits.

11 April 2018
Patrick Blower
Daily Telegraph

Donald Trump tweeted a warning that the American air force was about to attack Syria. 'Russia vows to shoot down any and all missiles fired at Syria,' he wrote: 'Get ready Russia, because they will be coming, nice and new and "smart!" You shouldn't be partners with a Gas Killing Animal who kills his people and enjoys it!' The US's decision to bomb Syria came in the wake of the deadly chemical weapons attack in Douma, Syria, which was widely attributed to the Syrian army.

13 April 2018
Steven Camley
Herald Scotland

Theresa May ordered British jets to bomb government chemical weapons plants in Syria. May commanded the RAF to join the air forces of the United States and France in the air strike, which came in retaliation for the previous week's chemical weapons attack in Douma. Vladimir Putin, an ally of Syrian premier Bashar al-Assad, said he condemned the US-led attack 'in the most serious way'. Here, Scott Clissold draws on Roy Lichtenstein's famous 1963 painting *Whaam!* to recreate the scene.

15 April 2018
Scott Clissold
Sunday Express

Amber Rudd, the home secretary, apologised for the 'appalling' treatment of post-war migrants to the UK, many of whom had been threatened with deportation. The controversy resulted from Theresa May's efforts to create a 'hostile environment' for illegal immigrants – efforts that had once involved sending a van marked 'Go home or face arrest' into high-migration areas. The scandal was particularly embarrassing for the government because it came almost exactly 50 years after the notorious 'Rivers of Blood' anti-immigration speech by Enoch Powell, here depicted sitting in the van's passenger seat.

18 April 2018
Steve Bell
Guardian

It was announced that Prince Charles would succeed the Queen as head of the Commonwealth. Commentators suggested the decision to confirm Charles may have been due to a personal intervention by the Queen, who had said it was her 'sincere wish' that her son take the position after her.

21 April 2018
Peter Brookes
The Times

PEACE TALKS

21 April 2018
Ingram Pinn
Financial Times

North Korean leader Kim Jong-un met with the US secretary of state, Mike Pompeo. The secret trip marked a major improvement in the relations of the two countries, whose leaders had been threatening one another with nuclear weapons only months beforehand. Donald Trump had previously described Kim as a 'maniac' and a 'madman', with Kim in turn calling Trump a 'rogue and gangster'.

Theresa May reiterated the government's commitment to leaving the EU's customs union. Jeremy Corbyn's Labour Party supported joining a new customs union after Brexit, causing May to lose a vote on the issue in the House of Lords. This image is a pastiche of a Leslie Illingworth cartoon from 1963, in which French premier Charles de Gaulle's elongated nose blocked Britain's entry into the European Economic Community.

24 April 2018
Dave Brown
Independent

"I wonder how they'll cope – now you only get benefits for the first two..."

24 April 2018
Steven Camley
Herald Scotland

The Duchess of Cambridge gave birth to her third child on 23 April. Prince Louis joined the British Royal Family as fifth in line to the throne. In other news, the High Court ruled that the government's 'two-child rule' – in which benefits are only paid for the first two children in a family – was legal.

Boris Johnson and Theresa May clashed over the treatment of post-war Commonwealth immigrants to the UK. The prime minister's migration policies had caused controversy after they led to longstanding British residents being deported and denied access to the health service. At a cabinet meeting, the foreign secretary, who notoriously once referred to Commonwealth citizens as 'flag-waving piccaninnies', called for an amnesty for all long-settled migrants to the UK.

26 April 2018
Steve Bell
Guardian

SPECIAL RELATIONSHIPS

28 April 2018
Ingram Pinn
Financial Times

Donald Trump brushed dandruff from the shoulder of the French president, Emmanuel Macron. 'We have a very special relationship – in fact, I'll get that little piece of dandruff off,' said the US president, as he touched Macron's suit in front of a crowd of reporters. Trump lavished praise on Macron throughout the visit, causing consternation among British commentators who thought it boded badly for the supposed UK–US 'special relationship'.

The home secretary, Amber Rudd, resigned. She had come under fire after telling MPs that she didn't know about Home Office deportation targets, whereas in fact she had received a memo on the policy. The original version of this cartoon (left) was drawn while Rudd was still in her position; the new caption (above) was hastily inserted after news broke about her resignation.

30 April 2018
Morten Morland
The Times

Having accepted Amber Rudd's resignation, Theresa May appointed the minister for communities and local government, Sajid Javid, as home secretary. Javid, the son of migrants from Pakistan, said he was 'angry' about the immigration scandal and said he would do 'whatever it takes' to make it right. But commentators continued to blame Theresa May for her government's migration policies, especially because many of them had been introduced while she was home secretary.

1 May 2018
Morten Morland
The Times

Donald Trump continued to publicly weigh up scrapping the US government's nuclear deal with Iran, leading to ever more public attempts by global leaders to influence his decision. On one side, Israel's Benjamin Netanyahu gave a theatrical presentation that was widely interpreted as an attempt to convince Trump to abandon the treaty. On the other, France's Emmanuel Macron and Britain's Theresa May made comments to the press calling for Trump to honour the deal.

3 May 2018
Kevin Kallaugher
Economist

5 May 2018
Ian Knox
Belfast Telegraph

Cambridge Analytica, the political consultancy alleged to have illicitly harvested online data on behalf of Donald Trump's supporters, announced that it was closing down due to mounting legal fees. The news came just weeks after a former Cambridge Analytica employee accused Leave.EU, the UKIP-linked Brexit campaign, of misusing data obtained from social media.

Donald Trump withdrew the United States from the Iran nuclear agreement. He said that the anti-nuclear proliferation deal, signed by President Barack Obama in 2015, was an 'embarrassment'. Trump's opponents said that he seemed to be pulling out of the agreement out of spite for Obama, rather than because he actually objected to its contents.

9 May 2018
Christian Adams
Evening Standard

The prime minister asked senior cabinet members including David Davis and Michael Gove to develop two detailed strategies for leaving the European Union, while the influential backbencher Jacob Rees-Mogg continued to criticise the government's approach. Meanwhile, the final of the Eurovision Song Contest – famously won by UK act Bucks Fizz in 1981 – took place in Portugal. Prophetically, this cartoon was published a month before Boris Johnson's now-infamous comment on businesses' concerns about Brexit: 'Fuck business,' he supposedly told a meeting of diplomats.

12 May 2018
Peter Brookes
The Times

Donald and Ivanka Trump attended the opening of the US embassy in Jerusalem, appearing alongside Israeli Prime Minister Benjamin Netanyahu. The embassy had controversially been relocated from Tel Aviv: Trump's critics said the move risked jeopardising the Arab–Israeli peace process, because Palestine does not recognise Israel's claim to Jerusalem.

15 May 2018
Morten Morland
The Times

16 May 2018
Christian Adams
Evening Standard

Theresa May was left isolated after she clashed with senior Conservatives over her Brexit strategy. Cabinet members disagreed over how best to approach leaving the European single market, with the prime minister's preferred policy coming under fire from the likes of Boris Johnson, Michael Gove and David Davis. Days later, May publicly quarrelled with backbencher Jacob Rees-Mogg over the implications of Brexit for the Irish border. Meanwhile, a new movie in the Star Wars franchise, *Solo: A Star Wars Story*, was released in British cinemas.

A report on building safety in the wake of the Grenfell Tower fire was branded a white-wash. The inquiry commissioned by the Conservative government found that there had been a 'race to the bottom' in building safety, but stopped short of recommending a ban on flammable cladding. Labour MP David Lammy criticised the decision, saying it was 'unthinkable and acceptable' that the cladding was still in use a year after the disaster.

18 May 2018
Steve Bell
Guardian

BURSTING BOLTON'S BUBBLE

19 May 2018
Ingram Pinn
Financial Times

Donald Trump's national security advisor, John Bolton, came under fire for calling for North Korea to adopt the 'Libya model' in abandoning its nuclear weapons programme. Kim Jong-un said that after denuclearising the Libyan regime had met a 'miserable fate', in which the US helped overthrow the government. The fracas raised concerns that the historic meeting scheduled between Kim and Trump would fall through.

Meghan Markle and her mother arrived at Cliveden House to spend the night ahead of the Royal Wedding. The bride-to-be had faced a turbulent start to the week, after her father was accused of setting up photos with the paparazzi. Her fiancé Prince Harry spent the night at Windsor Castle with the Queen and Duke of Edinburgh.

19 May 2018
Peter Brookes
The Times

20 May 2018
Nicola Jennings
Guardian

Donald Trump was criticised for his response to a school shooting in Santa Fe, Texas, in which 10 people were killed. Trump tweeted that he would 'grieve for the terrible loss of life', but stopped short of calling for greater gun control. His opponents said the president's understated response was down to his close links to the pro-gun lobby the National Rifle Association (NRA), and called on him to do more to prevent future shootings: 'Spare us your thoughts and prayers and do your job,' said the mayor of Dallas.

The leader of Windsor and Maidenhead Council asked police to clear the area of homeless people ahead of the Royal Wedding. Simon Dudley requested Thames Valley Police use their powers to counter an 'epidemic of rough sleeping and vagrancy in Windsor', writing, 'Obviously, the level of tourist interest is set to multiply with the royal wedding in May 2018, and there are increased concerns from our residents about their safety. The whole situation also presents a beautiful town in a sadly unfavourable light.'

20 May 2018
David Simonds
Observer

23 May 2018
Dave Brown
Independent

The former mayor of London Ken Livingstone resigned from the Labour Party. Livingstone had been plagued by allegations of antisemitism, which he denied, but said he was resigning because he had become a 'distraction' for the party.

BORIS FORCE ONE

We spend millions on Brexit a week
Let's fund a jet for **ME** too

Boris Johnson called for a private plane to help him promote the UK's interests around the world. Asked whether he needed a 'Brexit plane' to help him strike trade deals, the foreign secretary said, 'If there's a way of doing it that is not exorbitantly expensive then yes.' Johnson called for the plane to be decorated with a British flag. Christian Adams thought it would be more appropriate to emblazon it with a version of the slogan that appeared on the pro-Brexit campaign bus, 'We send the EU £350 million a week, let's fund our NHS instead'.

23 May 2018
Christian Adams
Evening Standard

28 May 2018
Patrick Blower
Daily Telegraph

The Republic of Ireland voted to legalise abortion in a referendum. The news put pressure on Theresa May, and Northern Ireland's first minister Arlene Foster, to reform abortion law north of the border – in Northern Ireland, abortion is illegal under almost all circumstances. The week also brought intense rain and lightning christened the 'mother of all thunderstorms' to the UK.

The future of Italy hung in the balance after the president vetoed a populist coalition between two parties, the 5-Star Movement and La Liga. President Sergio Mattarella refused to accept the alliance's proposed prime minister, Giuseppe Conte, because he had expressed opposition to the European single currency. Mattarella's decision left the country's political system at an *Italian Job*-style impasse, entrenching the stalemate between pro- and anti-EU factions in parliament.

29 May 2018
Patrick Blower
Daily Telegraph

BULLY-BOY BERCOW...

30 May 2018
Peter Brookes
The Times

The speaker of the House of Commons, John Bercow, faced calls to resign after a former employee accused him of bullying. His former private secretary, Angus Sinclair, said he had seen Bercow swear, shout and smash a phone while working in the speaker's office. Meanwhile, the *Sun* criticised the England footballer Raheem Sterling for getting a tattoo of an M16 assault rifle on his leg.

Ukraine faked the murder of a journalist in Kiev as part of an attempt to gather evidence on alleged Russian spies. A photo circulated on social media showing Arkady Babchenko lying facedown in a pool of blood, but he was subsequently revealed to be alive and well. In the UK, Theresa May – who was famously once pictured wearing a T-shirt saying 'This Is What a Feminist Looks Like' – came under fire from women's rights campaigners for backing down from abortion law reform in Northern Ireland. In the published version of this cartoon, the *Guardian* cropped out the left-hand panel, deeming it in poor taste.

1 June 2018
Steve Bell
Guardian

3 June 2018
Chris Riddell
Observer

Trade minister Liam Fox expressed concerns that Donald Trump would hike tariffs on imports of European cars. Fox, whose role involves forging post-Brexit trade relationships with foreign powers, warned that Trump's protectionism would have a negative impact on British manufacturers. He said that Theresa May would raise the issue with Trump at the upcoming meeting of G7 leaders.

'Gimme a room or the dog gets it!'

The police reopened an investigation into the attempted murder of the lover of the former Liberal Party politician Jeremy Thorpe. The announcement came after the press revealed that Andrew Norton – the alleged would-be assassin in the case, who reportedly shot Thorpe's lover's dog – might still be alive and resident in the UK. The renewed interest in the case arose from a BBC drama about the case, *A Very English Scandal.*

5 June 2018
Stan McMurtry
Daily Mail

Transport Secretary Chris Grayling apologised for the severe delays to the rail network in northern England, following the roll-out of a new timetable. According to the cartoonist, 'This was my personal take on how I perceive Chris Grayling and his apathetic and sluggish attempts to arrest the Northern Rail Network crisis! The *Yorkshire Post* has continually challenged him over this and he chooses to go into hiding!'

5 June 2018
Graeme Bandeira
Yorkshire Post

IN MEMORY OF RAZAN AL·NAJJAR — NOT

Theresa May hosted Israel's prime minister, Benjamin Netanyahu, at 10 Downing Street. Steve Bell's cartoon incorporates a famous image of Razan al-Najjar, a Palestinian nurse who was killed during protests in Gaza in 2018. In the original version of the cartoon al-Najjar was on fire inside the hearth, but this image was rejected by *Guardian* editor Katharine Viner because it 'conjured up an image of the Holocaust'. Bell criticised the decision, saying he was being 'unfairly traduced and censored'. The following day he submitted the above, amended image – featuring al-Najjar in the sights of a sniper rifle – but the *Guardian* said it was too late for it to be published.

7 June 2018
Steve Bell
***Guardian* (unpublished)**

Donald Trump met with the leader of North Korea, Kim Jong-un. The two men got on unexpectedly well, with Trump later describing Kim as 'a very talented man'. Trump's other diplomatic engagement of the week was more fraught: he pulled out of a joint statement by the G7 group of nations on issues including trade and national security, following a tumultuous meeting with leaders including Canada's Justin Trudeau, Germany's Angela Merkel and France's Emmanuel Macron. Meanwhile, in the UK, viewers were hooked on a new series of the ITV2 reality show *Love Island*.

11 June 2018
Christian Adams
Evening Standard

Jeremy Corbyn was accused of hypocrisy over his approach to Brexit, after the Labour Party said that it supported remaining in a European 'internal market'. Corbyn's critics argued the announcement was a betrayal to Leave voters, who they say had envisaged a cleaner break with the EU. According to the *Sun*'s Trevor Kavanagh, Corbyn's decision was an 'unscrupulous bid . . . to ride to power as Britain's first full-blown Marxist Prime Minister'.

11 June 2018
Steve Bright
Sun

147

SUMMIT SHOWDOWN

12 June 2018
Patrick Blower
Daily Telegraph

Theresa May called for unity in the Conservative Party in the build-up to a series of crucial votes on her EU Withdrawal Bill. The government's Brexit legislation had been criticised by 'hard Brexit' advocates like Boris Johnson and Jacob Rees-Mogg, as well as by pro-Europe figures like Anna Soubry. Here, Patrick Blower recreates a photo from the G7 summit (right) that captured Donald Trump frowning while encircled by a group of world leaders.

In the wake of Donald Trump's historic meeting with Kim Jong-un, the two leaders signed an agreement committing to improve their relationship, in accordance with 'the desire of the peoples of the two countries for peace and prosperity'. Commentators pointed out the remarkable shift in tone from the previous year, when the two leaders had publicly clashed, and Trump had ridiculed Kim as a 'rocket man' on a 'suicide mission' (see p. 11).

15 June 2018
Gerald Scarfe
Evening Standard

RUSSIA 2018

16 June 2018
Ben Jennings
i

A ceremony in Moscow marked the beginning of the 2018 FIFA World Cup. Russian president Vladimir Putin said that he wanted to host an 'open, hospitable and friendly' tournament. However, critics of the Kremlin said that Putin was likely to use the event as an opportunity to demonstrate Russia's power to the world.

Theresa May announced a £20 billion per year funding boost for the NHS. The prime minister said it would be partly funded by a 'Brexit dividend' – evoking memories of the famous promise of £350 million per week for the NHS emblazoned on the Leave campaign bus – but her critics said it would inevitably require tax rises. According to the cartoonist, 'When I started to work on this I thought I might avoid the red bus. I felt it had been done too many times. But then if you are going to tell great big whoppers you really shouldn't leave such great big whopping evidence behind. So it was too good to ignore. I love drawing Michael Gove and Boris Johnson together. A classic double act in the Laurel and Hardy tradition. Except it isn't funny.'

18 June 2018
Peter Schrank
The Times

20 June 2018
Steven Camley
Herald Scotland

Donald Trump abandoned his policy of splitting up families caught entering America illegally. The White House had tightened its guidelines on illegal immigration in April, leading to thousands of children being taken from their parents at the US–Mexico border – with many being held in 'cages' by immigration forces. The policy was part of the Trump administration's 'zero tolerance' approach to illegal immigration, which also involves the plans for the long-promised wall between the US and Mexico.

The former leader of the Conservative Party, William Hague, called for recreational cannabis use to be legalised. In an article published in the *Daily Telegraph*, the Tory peer said that the government's policy was 'inappropriate, ineffective and utterly out of date'. But Theresa May's government rejected Hague's suggestion, saying, 'The penalties for the illicit possession, cultivation and trafficking of cannabis will remain the same.'

20 June 2018
Patrick Blower
Evening Standard

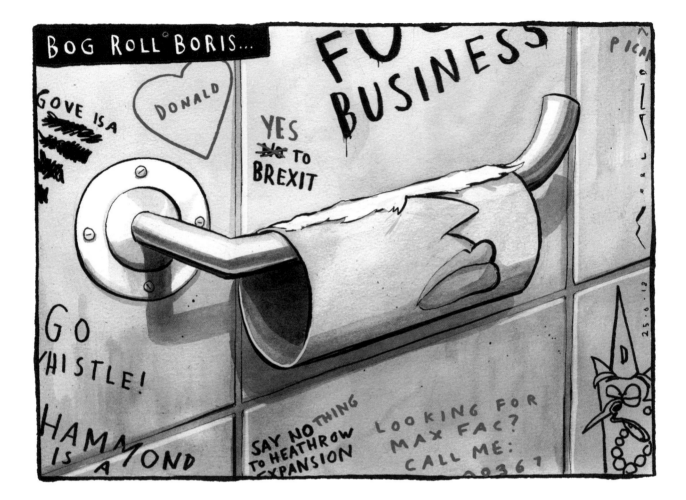

25 June 2018
Morten Morland
The Times

Boris Johnson said Britain should avoid a 'bog roll Brexit' that is 'soft, yielding and seemingly indefinitely long'. The foreign secretary's comments came in a *Sun* article in which he advocated a quick and clean break with Europe. Days later the government entered a new round of negotiations with the EU, in which they continued to discuss the future customs relationship.

Treasury minister Liz Truss publicly mocked the environment secretary, Michael Gove, over his plans to protect the environment. Truss said that his proposed regulations on wood-burning stoves – or 'wood-burning Goves', as she called them – were an example of 'hot air' coming from the Department for Environment, Food and Rural Affairs.

28 June 2018
Dave Brown
Independent

30 June 2018
Ben Jennings
i

A report found that the UK was complicit in the 'inexcusable' mistreatment of terror suspects. A report by the Intelligence and Security Committee of Parliament alleged that in the wake of 9/11, British security agencies supplied intelligence to their allies, despite knowing of more than 200 cases in which they had mistreated and water-boarded detainees.

Reality TV show *Love Island* became the most-watched show ever to be broadcast on ITV2. According to the cartoonist, 'Tory *Love Island*. The contestants: Boris and Esther, Sajid and Andrea – they're wearing skimpy swimwear and they're hot for Brexit.'

1 July 2018
Chris Riddell
Observer

1 July 2018
Scott Clissold
Sunday Express

Chancellor Angela Merkel struggled to reassert her authority in the wake of criticism from within and outside Germany. Throughout the summer she had come under fire from her Bavarian coalition partners, and from the leaders of EU countries including Italy and Hungary, for her supposedly lenient policy towards migrants.

CABINET DISCIPLINE IN SHREDS

MAY'S for BRE

PLAN XIT

Theresa May's attempts to finalise the Brexit policy White Paper were undermined by criticisms from within the cabinet. Environment Secretary Michael Gove allegedly tore up a government report on plans for a new partnership with the EU after Brexit, while Boris Johnson reportedly said he would fight Theresa May's 'soft Brexit', 'and win'. Fellow Brexiteers including David Davis and Liam Fox were also reported to have reservations about the government's approach.

2 July 2018
Nicola Jennings
Guardian

6 July 2018
Peter Brookes
The Times

A man and woman were found unconscious in Wiltshire following exposure to the nerve agent Novichok. The police said the pair's symptoms indicated they had touched the same chemical that nearly killed ex-Russian spy Sergei Skripal in April – suggesting that Vladimir Putin's Kremlin may have been involved in the poisoning.

Donald Trump took to Twitter to criticise his allies in the military alliance NATO. 'The United States is spending far more on Nato than any other Country,' he wrote. 'This is not fair, nor is it acceptable.' According to the cartoonist, 'This has got to be one of the oldest visual gags in the book. Sometimes it's fun to try and breathe new life into an old idea.'

7 July 2018
Peter Schrank
Economist

In a fraught cabinet summit, Theresa May secured government backing for her plan to create a 'free trade area' with Europe. Pro-Brexit members of the government including Boris Johnson, David Davis and Michael Gove had argued that the scheme effectively amounted to remaining in the European single market. In other news, England manager Gareth Southgate exceeded all expectations when his team qualified for the semi-finals of the FIFA World Cup.

8 July 2018
Scott Clissold
Sunday Express

The influential pro-Brexit MP Jacob Rees-Mogg said that Theresa May's Chequers plan for Brexit would be worse for Britain than a 'no-deal' with the EU. 'As with eggs: an egg that is very softly boiled isn't boiled at all,' he said. 'A very soft Brexit means that we haven't left, we are simply a rule taker. That is not something that this country voted for, it is not what the Prime Minister promised.'

8 July 2018
Brian Adcock
Independent

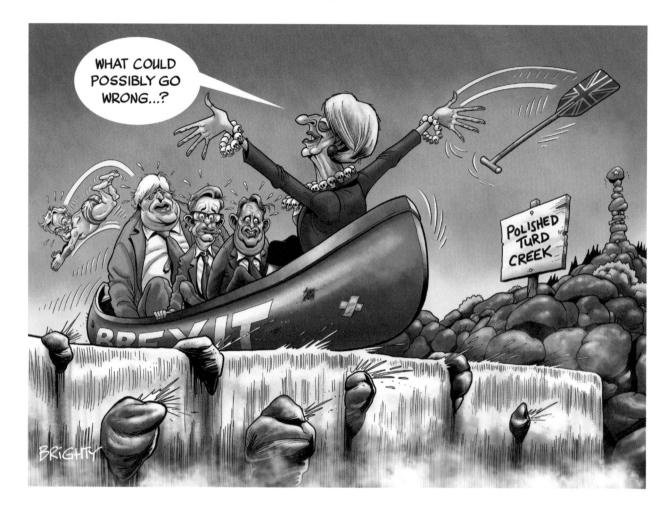

9 July 2018
Steve Bright
Sun

Brexit Secretary David Davis resigned over Theresa May's new Brexit plan. In his resignation letter, Davis said it seemed 'less and less likely' that Britain would leave the European customs union and single market. The press also reported that the foreign secretary, Boris Johnson, had described May's proposal for a new 'free trade area' as 'polishing a turd' during the cabinet meeting at Chequers.

Boris Johnson resigned as foreign secretary, just hours after David Davis quit as Brexit secretary. According to the cartoonist, 'I woke up to news that a minister had resigned and started drawing this [right]. Lunchtime, ahead of schedule, I popped out for half an hour and came back to find another one had gone and some redrawing was in order. Maybe I should pop out more often.'

10 July 2018
Dave Brown
Independent

14 July 2018
Peter Brookes
The Times

Donald Trump criticised Theresa May's Brexit plan. He told the *Sun* that her plan to forge a new 'free trade area' with Europe would 'wreck' Brexit, saying, 'I would have done it much differently'. Over the Channel, activists planned their protests for Trump's visit to the UK: a crowd-funding campaign to create a blimp that depicted Trump as a nappy-clad baby raised £29,000.

Democratic Unionist MP Ian Paisley faced suspension from the House of Commons after he failed to declare the details of two family holidays in 2013 paid for by the Sri Lankan government. Paisley, who is reportedly on good terms with Donald Trump, was criticised by MPs for his links with the Sri Lankan state, which has been accused of locking up its political opponents and other human rights abuses.

20 July 2018
Ian Knox
Belfast Telegraph

22 July 2018
Scott Clissold
Sunday Express

Donald Trump invited Vladimir Putin to visit the White House. The invitation sparked controversy in the US, where Trump was under fire for failing to criticise Russia's foreign policy at a press conference in Helsinki four days previously: the president had said that he 'didn't see any reason' the Kremlin would have tried to influence American politics, despite the CIA and FBI having found extensive evidence of Russian meddling.

Dominic Raab said that Britain would refuse to pay its £39 billion 'divorce bill' to the EU if the two failed to reach a trade deal. In an interview with the *Sunday Telegraph*, the new Brexit secretary said that the payment was conditional on Brussels 'fulfilling its side of the bargain'. Raab's comments came just days after his first meeting with the EU's chief negotiator, Michel Barnier.

23 July 2018
Brian Adcock
Independent

25 July 2018
Christian Adams
Evening Standard

Theresa May played down fears of food shortages in the event of a no-deal Brexit. Newspapers had reported that the government was planning to stockpile food and medicine, in preparation for disruptions to the supply chain brought about by a 'hard Brexit'. But the prime minister said that people should take 'reassurance and comfort' from the policy, because it showed the government was preparing 'for every eventuality'.

'Don't interfere! Er... the sun must have bleached ours.'

Theresa May took direct control of Britain's Brexit negotiations with the EU, reducing the power of the newly appointed Brexit secretary, Dominic Raab. Under the new arrangement, the 'Europe Unit' led by the senior civil servant Olly Robbins had 'overall responsibility for the preparation and conduct of the negotiations', and reported directly to the prime minister. Pro-Brexit commentators said the reorganisation indicated that May was getting ready to give in to the EU's demands.

26 July 2018
Stan McMurtry
Daily Mail

26 July 2018
Christian Adams
Evening Standard

After months of mounting tensions over trade policy, Donald Trump came to an agreement with European Commission President Jean-Claude Juncker about the need for a 'zero-tariff' arrangement between the EU and America. Commentators said the newfound cosiness between the two powers left Theresa May isolated. Meanwhile, the longest heatwave in living memory continued to break records across Europe.

Theresa May began a week-long walking holiday in Italy. The break came after weeks of mounting tensions over Brexit: the prime minister faced calls to take a more hard-line approach with Brussels from some MPs, while others called for another referendum on leaving the EU.

29 July 2018
Scott Clissold
Sunday Express

31 July 2018
Andy Davey
Telegraph

Several MPs accused Jeremy Corbyn of turning a blind eye to anti-semitism in the Labour Party. According to the cartoonist, 'Two Labour MPs, Margaret Hodge and Ian Austin, were being investigated over the growing wave of discomfort over the way the anti-Semitism row in Labour was being handled (or not) by Jeremy Corbyn. He seemed to be happily surfing on a small, calm wave of his own, while behind him is a huge tidal wave. Could this be his breaker?'

As the hottest summer on record wore on, Theresa May cut short her holiday to hold emergency Brexit talks with Emmanuel Macron. May's approach, based on the 'Chequers plan' outlined in July, had been attacked as unrealistic by the French premier. May's visit to Macron's summer home was ridiculed in the French press, with one newspaper describing it as a 'cry for help'.

3 August 2018
Christian Adams
Evening Standard

BALLOT BATTLES

4 August 2018
Ingram Pinn
Financial Times

Six people were killed in protests over alleged vote-rigging in the Zimbabwean election. The police opened fire on supporters of the opposition party, Movement for Democratic Change, whose leader said that the government's victory was 'fraudulent'. As the first vote since the ousting of Robert Mugabe, the election had been intended to set Zimbabwe on a new path following years of repressive rule.

Blower 6.8.18 - After Illingworth. blowercartoons.com

The EU's chief Brexit negotiator, Michel Barnier, said he would not compromise in his approach to Theresa May's plan for leaving the EU. Whitehall officials had hoped that Brussels would soften its stance, in the wake of rumours that the UK was preparing for a 'no-deal' Brexit. Patrick Blower's cartoon is based on an earlier one by Leslie Illingworth, published during the Cuban Missile Crisis, which depicted US President John F. Kennedy and Soviet premier Nikita Khrushchev arm wrestling while sitting on hydrogen bombs. It appeared on 29 October 1962 in the *Daily Mail*.

6 August 2018
Patrick Blower
Daily Telegraph

7 August 2018
Morten Morland
The Times

International trade minister Liam Fox said that the chance of a no-deal Brexit was growing. Blaming the 'intransigence' of the EU, Fox said that European officials had dismissed Theresa May's Brexit strategy simply because they 'have never done it before'. Remainers reacted angrily to Fox's comments, pointing to his statement during the Leave campaign that a trade deal with Europe would be 'one of the easiest in human history'.

According to the cartoonist, 'Boris Johnson was accused of "fanning the flames of Islamophobia" after saying that Muslim women who wear veils look like "bank robbers" and "letter boxes". Mr Bean (alias Rowan Atkinson) stepped into the burqa debate by saying that Boris should be allowed to mock religion. Yes, Atkinson has a point, and no, the burqa is by no means a flag of feminist or religious freedom – but it seems unlikely that Boris started it all up in order to create a clearer space for satire.'

10 August 2018
Andy Davey
Evening Standard

PRESENT BUT NOT INVOLVED

Blower 14.8.18 blowercartoons.com

14 August 2018
Patrick Blower
Daily Telegraph

Jeremy Corbyn admitted he had been present at a wreath-laying for the alleged perpetrators of a 1972 terrorist attack on Israeli athletes, but claimed, 'I don't think I was actually involved in it.' Photographs of the Labour leader holding a wreath in the Palestinian Martyrs' Cemetery in Tunisia had surfaced, following months of criticism over his supposed links with militant groups such as the IRA and Hamas. Meanwhile, Boris Johnson emerged from his house to offer cups of tea to tired journalists. The press had been stationed outside his Oxfordshire home to quiz him on his controversial comments about Muslim women.

I'M ONLY HERE TO LAY A WREATH FOR MR CORBYN!

PALESTINE R.I.P.

Benjamin Netanyahu criticised Jeremy Corbyn over his attendance at an event honouring alleged Palestinian terrorists. The Israeli prime minister tweeted, 'The laying of a wreath by Jeremy Corbyn on the graves of the terrorists who perpetrated the Munich massacre and his comparison of Israel to the Nazis deserves unequivocal condemnation from everyone – left, right and everything in between.' Jeremy Corbyn hit back by saying what deserved 'unequivocal condemnation' was 'the killing of over 160 Palestinian protesters in Gaza by Israeli forces since March, including dozens of children'.

15 August 2018
Dave Brown
Independent

Economists predicted that rail fares would rise by 3.5 per cent in 2019. The announcement sparked anger among commuters, who had already experienced a summer of chaos during which changes to the rail timetable had led to hundreds of cancellations. Railway unions said that the government was underinvesting in long-needed improvements to the system, and that train staff were underpaid and demoralised.

16 August 2018
Seamus Jennings
Daily Telegraph

HE'S BACK, AGAIN.....

LEAVE MEANS LEAVE

RETIRED MEANS RETIRED

Less than two years after 'retiring' from frontline politics, Nigel Farage said he was returning to campaign against Theresa May's 'fraudulent' Brexit plan. The former UKIP leader
said he would be part of a 'battle bus' tour by the lobby group Leave Means Leave, which
opposes the prime minister's proposals for a 'soft Brexit'.

19 August 2018
Brian Adcock
Independent

Rudy Giuliani, Donald Trump's lawyer, claimed that 'truth isn't truth' in a television interview. Giuliani made his comments to NBC after host Chuck Todd pressed him on whether Trump should testify to the investigation into Russian interference in the 2016 presidential election. 'When you tell me that he should testify because he's going to tell the truth and he shouldn't worry, well that's so silly because it's somebody's version of the truth. Not *the* truth,' said Giuliani.

21 August 2018
Dave Brown
Independent

Donald Trump's former lawyer, Michael Cohen, told a court that he had been instructed to pay the porn-star Stormy Daniels $130,000 to silence her claims of an affair with the president. Cohen's statement came just minutes after another former Trump ally, Paul Manafort, was found guilty of fraud – a prosecution that arose from the investigation into the Trump campaign's alleged links with Russian agents. Commentators suggested the developments could undermine the Republican Party's performance in the November mid-term elections, but Trump dismissed the news as a 'Russian witch hunt'.

26 August 2018
Chris Riddell
Observer

27 August 2018
Steve Bright
Sun

Labour Party moderates met for a barbecue at Peter Mandelson's house in London. The *Sunday Times* reported that the event was attended by around ten MPs from the right of the party, including deputy leader Tom Watson, and involved discussions about the future of the Labour movement. Jeremy Corbyn loyalists said that the event would only pour oil on the simmering tensions within the party.

Pope Francis said he was ashamed of the Catholic Church's response to the 'repellent crimes' of sex abuse committed by its clergymen. Speaking during the first papal visit to Ireland in four decades, Francis said the 'failure' of ecclesiastical authorities to address the allegations 'remains a source of pain and shame for the Catholic community'. But critics said that, in the absence of a concrete plan to tackle sexual abuse, the pope's words rung hollow.

27 August 2018
David Simonds
The Times

29 August 2018
Steve Bell
Guardian

Theresa May claimed that failing to reach a Brexit deal with the EU 'wouldn't be the end of the world'. Acknowledging that no-deal 'wouldn't be a walk in the park', the prime minister nonetheless distanced herself from Treasury forecasts that suggested a no-deal Brexit would cost the Exchequer an extra £80 billion in borrowing. Here, Steve Bell paints a rather bleaker picture, recreating John Martin's apocalyptic painting *The Great Day of His Wrath* (1851–3).

Vladimir Putin backtracked on a controversial plan to make changes to the state pension. The Russian leader appeared on television to announce that the retirement age for women would rise to 60, instead of to 63 as had been planned. The president himself, turning 66 in October, seems to have no plans to retire.

30 August 2018
Peter Brookes
The Times

ROBBEN ISLAND . . .

FREE
NELSON
MANDELA
GAFFE
WITH EVERY
INTERVIEW

30 August 2018
Dave Brown
Independent

On a visit to South Africa, Theresa May faced questions about her stance on apartheid during the 1970s and 1980s. In an interview with Channel 4 News, the prime minister was pressed on whether she had ever agreed with the former Conservative leader Margaret Thatcher that Nelson Mandela was a 'terrorist'. The tense encounter took place just hours before May visited Robben Island, the former prison where Mandela spent two decades.

'On second thoughts I won't have the scallops, I'll try the prawn cocktail'

The UK government backed British fishermen embroiled in a cross-Channel row over scallop fishing. About 40 French boats had tried to stop Britons from working off the Normandy coast, alleging that UK fishermen were depleting shellfish stocks too early in the season. But Michael Gove said that the British boats had 'every right to be in those waters'.

31 August 2018
Stan McMurtry
Daily Mail

31 August 2018
Gerald Scarfe
Evening Standard

Alex Salmond, the former leader of the Scottish National Party, resigned from the party amid allegations of sexual misconduct. The previous week it had emerged that two Scottish government staff members had lodged complaints about Salmond's behaviour when he was Scotland's first minister. Salmond said that the claims about him were 'patently ridiculous', but that he wanted to prevent internal divisions emerging within the SNP.